WHAT'S YOUR VIBE?

KAT MAJIK

This is a work of fiction. Names, characters, places, and situations are the product of the author's imagination, or are used fictitiously.

this one's for all of you who are just trying
to figure your stuff out, man
(...she says, with the wry, mildly self-deprecatory amusement
of someone who's been there, and occasionally still is)

PREFACE

"You write about what you love and you write
about things you're trying to make sense of."
—Bruce Springsteen

The fun thing about writing a demisexual romance is that even
I—tried-and-true demisexual dum-dum (lollipop)—don't know
if I'm explaining it right. The technical definition is "a person
who experiences sexual feelings and attraction only after de-
veloping a close emotional relationship, and not on the basis of
first impressions, physical characteristics, etc."

That might help. But! I'm not trying to change the world here
(I'm just. Too tired. Maybe it's an iron deficiency, but *anyway*...).

Mostly I thought this story would be funny, and sweet, and I
could explain the way I feel about love in a way that might make
other people understand what I mean, and might make some
others understand themselves, too.

In my own journey into the queer experience, sexuality has
existed on a spectrum. I've found that there are always going to
be exceptions and outliers and things that confuse you into an
identity crisis.

Labels aren't a box you're not allowed to leave—they're just one piece of your puzzle, a means to *start* understanding and accepting yourself, but not The Thing to live and die by.

You contain multitudes, babe! Don't let how you think you're "*supposed to* be" dictate what you're allowed to want.

So anyway... That's enough vulnerability for one author's note, so! In other hodgepodge news:

- While there are some familiar Indiana landmarks within, the town itself is fictional.

- If you recognize any of the jokes, etc., from a fanfic, don't sweat it; I probably wrote that fanfic.

- Yes indeedy, the sex shop information and stories are true—both factually (like how to clean your toys) and, alas and woe is me and so on, autobiographically (like how I was repeatedly and tragically disheartened by the state of humanity whenever someone got stuck in their penis pump). I did give some of these hilariously sordid tales a little zhuzh for the plot, but they're all, at the very least, *based* in reality.

- Keep an eye out for the chapter about porn titles. I only made up two of them (and those almost certainly exist, anyway, in some variation), and you're prooooooobably not gonna guess which ones.

...I think that covers it. Happy reading! xo —Maj

"It's not exactly love at first sight.
It is more like soul recognition."

—Lynette Simeone

Contents

A CRISIS OF SEXUAL IDENTITY

The last thing Milo wants to do at ten-thirty in the morning is explain, *repeatedly*, why you shouldn't try to stick an anal vibrator up your girlfriend's vag.

But, well... Man plans, God laughs.

He'll laugh, too. *Later*, after he can finish his emotional support breakfast Pepsi. But first things first, gotta prevent a trip to the OR.

Alas. Such is the life of a sex shop customer service rep.

"If you stick this"—he flourishes the package—"up in her business, you're going to die alone."

Erik—a regular customer who does indeed *regularly* say the stupidest shit Milo's ever heard in his otherwise unremarkable thirty years—*simpers* at him, like *Milo's* the one who thinks the purpose of an anal vibrator isn't precisely what it says it is.

"Well, if I can get it in, I'll be able to get it out."

(*You see?!* Stupid.)

"Uh, sure. Said every kid who's ever gotten their head stuck in a banister." Yes, Milo is *well aware* that the vagina has more natural elasticity than *oak* or *stainless steel* or... *whatever*, he's not an architect. But this conversation has been going in circles for like six solid minutes, alright, at this point it's the principle of the thing.

"Erik. My dude. My man. My guy. Seriously, we have actual vaginal vibrators for, y'know, *vaginas*. Vulvas, the mons pubis, that *entire* kit and caboodle."

Usually he'd get more specific—you've got your external, internal, dual, clitoral, the whole shebang (pun only slightly intended)—but he'd bet his favorite scrunchie (the navy one with the cartoon mushrooms, currently and unsuccessfully tying back his riot of curls that aren't *quite* long enough for a scrunchie, anyway) that this guy doesn't know the difference.

In fact he *knows* that Erik doesn't know the difference; no, sir, Erik looks like he was made in a wax museum—seriously, his facial symmetry is *uncanny*—and he thinks that's all he needs to pick up girls, and that they'll stick around regardless of what he sticks *inside of her*.

Milo would blame the American school system, but Erik's like, twenty-six. He's an adult. At a certain point you just have to start Googling this shit, man.

"Wait a second." Milo squints. He's never sure if it achieves the desired effect, because while he does have some *dreamboat* brown eyes, if he does say so himself, the slight cross of the left one—aka strabismus, specifically esotropia, and no he *can't* do anything about it—makes him look entirely unthreatening (this is Cookie Monster's fault, somehow). Oh, well.

"Whose vagina is this for? Is it someone you're mad at, is that what this is about? Because you can't do that."

Erik squints right back at him, and God damn his 20/20 perfectly aligned baby blues, ugh, what *is* that? "You gotta start watching something that's not SVU."

"There are over *five hundred* episodes. *And counting.* Who's got time for something else?" Milo hooks the vibrator back on its slightly loose rack. "I'm not selling you that."

"So what would you recommend?"

"I'd *recommend* you ask the girl you're dating what she's into." Milo doesn't tend to grasp at the clientele's sexuality straws, but Erik is notoriously straight (derogatory, because he's a dick about it).

Milo swipes his room-temp Pepsi off the counter, throws it back like a shot. "Or are you doing that thing where you don't talk to her about it? Can't be doing that, either, dude."

"What's there to talk about?" Erik wants to know, but also has no actual interest in knowing. They've danced this dance before, baby, Milo's heard it all. "I *get* pussy, man, I think I know what I'm doing."

Oh, what the fuck ever. Just because he "*gets pussy*" doesn't mean he knows what to do with it. Sure, Milo doesn't have the... *experience*... to talk, but in his humble opinion as someone with far more self-awareness than the Eriks of the world, your track record doesn't count for shit when you don't pay attention to your trackees.

Everyone is different—their bodies, their turn-ons, sexual pleasure isn't one-size-fits-all. Even if you do manage to get someone off by sheer force of your own self-inflated ego, that's just biology; their body might feel good—*stimulated*—but that doesn't mean *they* feel good.

But, hey, turns out Erik might not even know where he's sticking it, so. Probably a waste of time to stand here with him, digging into the emotional ramifications of sex.

"Sure. You're a real connoisseur." Milo slurps obnoxiously at his pop. "Still not selling you an anal toy for vaginal use, though."

Erik relents like he always does, thank God for small miracles, and leaves five minutes later with a pack of condoms. Gonna do fuck-all for Milo's commission, but he still has his integrity. Or maybe it's more like a perverse sense of self-righteousness? Whichever. At least he can finish his Pepsi in peace, nothing but stocking merch to keep them apart now.

Twelve boxes and fifteen pages of inventory to match it against, to be exact. The utter and devastating mundanity of it all is probably why the corporate radio is pop hits of the '80s, '90s, *and Today!* Nothing gets you off your ass like "If I Could Turn Back Time," *thank you,* Cher.

(It certainly puts Milo in a better mood than something like, say, "Crimson and Clover." The last time he heard *that,* it was beneath the harsh fluorescents smack in the middle of the frozen pizza aisle, elevenish P.M., and *all he was trying to do, for the love of God,* was weigh the merits of spending $7.99 on brand name versus $2.99 on the budget stuff, *not* have an impromptu existential crisis about falling in love. He's still not sure what he could have possibly done to Tommy James & the Shondells to have been so *personally attacked,* but clearly it was *something.*)

Ah, there's the first exploded lube bottle of today's shipment. It's the silicone stuff, horrendously sticky. Not even one of the edible ones, so Milo can't reasonably—though, eh, probably still not super sanitary—lick it off his hand and get on with his day.

And lo, the perils of big business strike again.

Though, really, Nobody's Secret—Milo continues to find this hilarious, by the way—isn't exactly *big business.* The pay is still peanuts, commission notwithstanding, but the discount's good (forty percent off, can't complain) and so are the hours (except for the surprise double shifts, ten A.M. to midnight, when the newbies decide they can't hack it, after all, and pull a no-call, no-show, which happens, ooooh... *literally all the time*).

It's a small shop paneled in fake wood, innocuous enough in the front: lingerie, wedding bits-and-bobs; and then things progress from there: massage oils, lubes, onto the toys, and then the DVDs and BDSM such-and-such in the back.

People usually do a lap before they loosen up enough to *peruse*. That's the small-town Midwest for you. A church on every other corner, every iteration of fast food and way too many stop signs, and a mass case of Catholic guilt (sometimes the guilt's more nondenominational Christian, but that doesn't roll off the tongue as nicely).

Maybe that's why Cooper, the manager, is on an endless crusade to get everyone to stop calling it a sex shop. It's bad for the *image*, he says, as if they don't stock products like the *Homewrecker* and *Co-ed Cumslut* and that ever-present copy of grandpa kink (you heard that right) on the porn shelf.

There's nothing morally wrong with any of that—though, yeah, okay, so Milo's got his reservations about the grandpa thing—but *sex shop* covers it just as well as adult novelties or adult boutique or adult some-other-vague-noun.

They got their spot in the strip mall with the laundromat, the taco place, the smoothie bar, that insurance company that's probably a front for something, and the store with all the fancy lampshades that is *staunchly* religious (closed on Sundays to "celebrate the true LIGHT of Our Lord and Savior"), with *nary* a protestation—not even from the fancy lampshade people!—so why fix what ain't broken?

They're called *Nobody's Secret*, hello, everybody already *knows*.

Milo's worked here for five years, something to supplement his part-time mechanic income, because part-time's the best they can give him. He does pretty well, between the two, and he has no plans to ditch either. The whole strabismus thing, according to his ophthalmologist, can make it hard to land a job—apparently a cross-eye doesn't make the greatest first impression, but it's not like potential employers have to disclose their ableism, ha cha cha cha cha—so Milo's certainly not going to dip out of the ones he has.

Artemis swings by around noon to drop off a burrito bowl and, why not, paint his nails. He's on staycation and everyone else is at work, the store's usually dead around now, anyhow, and you can't argue with a roommate who brings you Chipotle. But Milo's natural inclination to the side-eye is giving him a run for his money.

"Do you have to do that here?"

"Yeah." Artemis blows on the coat of jewel-bright blue he just applied. He leans back in the chair behind the counter, props his vintage ankle boots next to the register. "My nail place is booked, where am I supposed to go?"

"Uh. *Home?*" Milo suggests, as he scans racks to input their next order. The glow-in-the-dark dildos are *quite* the selling point; everyone loves a good aesthetic, huh.

"Why, so you can have another unnecessary bout of the *vapors* when I spill nail polish on the carpet?" Artemis rolls his dark eyes. "We *rent* that place, bimbo."

"Right. Which is why I don't want you spilling shit on the carpet."

"You were *bedridden* about it."

"Bah." Milo waves his hands around, then resumes scanning (despite his personal aversion to a vibrator fashioned in the likeness of the *pickle emoji*—not to kinkshame or anything, but *Christ* if he understands the next generation...). He wasn't *actually* bedridden, by the way; but, yeah, maybe he had an emotional overreaction, otherwise known as just a *slight* panic attack, when Artemis knocked this garish red stuff all over the apartment's standard-issue cream carpeting.

That was in the early days of their friendship, a few years ago when Milo couldn't take living with his parents anymore—he loves them, he does, but his dad doesn't rinse his dishes and *that's how families fall apart, man*—but who can afford rent, right?

Most of his friends were coupled up, all very high school sweethearts about it (and they're still going strong, which seems statistically improbable, but there you go). They were doing the whole nuclear family thing, so, whatever, Milo was on to other options.

At that point—hell, even now—Milo didn't understand how Craigslist worked and he was too afraid to ask, so he went swiping for a roommate on Tinder. A little off-beat, sure, but roll with the times.

He'd matched (and blessedly quick, too) with Artemis Bello, dark-skinned and big-smiled, who has really good eyebrows that are slightly arched over gold-rimmed glasses. The dude's all old-school swagger in his pinstripes and suspenders, and his pocket squares always complement his nail polish. His own curls were far better groomed than whatever Milo was doing with his 3-in-1 shampoo.

One stipulation of their roommate agreement was, in fact, that he *stop using that*, and Milo is a better person for it.

Artemis is five years older and, even back then, established at his job in promotional marketing for restaurants, bars, the works. He didn't *need* a roommate, but he says living alone is depressing and something white people do to themselves for no reason.

He slid into Milo's DMs entirely matter-of-fact, potentially hurtful if Milo had an ego problem: *You're not even a little bit my type. We could make a roomie situation work without getting all CW teen drama about it. Wanna meet for smoothies?*

Badda bing, badda boom, they've been living together ever since.

When Artemis starts applying a second coat of polish, Milo groans, exaggerated to make his point. "You're not supposed to be back there."

"Oh, yeah? What are you gonna do, tell Cooper?" Artemis brandishes the brush dismissively. "Please. I'm gonna start charging that man OnlyFans money every time he looks at me with that gleam of 'no homo' crisis in his eyes, then we could both quit our jobs."

"Man—" Milo shakes his head, scans a near-empty rack of tongue vibrators (which is what Erik *should* have bought this morning, but his grasp on cunnilingus is... up in the air, at best). "I legitimately do not know where you got the idea that Cooper's into you."

"Oh, and what's *that* supposed to mean? Am I not good enough for your boss and his tacky sports coat?"

"Is it tacky?" Milo pictures it, in all its admittedly ugly glory. "I thought it was just, like, metallic?"

"Same thing. Who does he think he is? A Spice Girl? Ha!" Artemis waggles his fingers, again dismissively. "I could wear that. He can't pull it off."

"I can't keep having this conversation with you."

"You're the one who insists there's nothing wrong with his coat. Why is he always wearing that?"

"Professionalism?"

"*Delusion.*"

Okay, fine, so this really is Milo's fault, for challenging the status quo that everyone wants to bang and/or get banged by Artemis. And, to be fair, most people do. History goes to show that, whether it's his own or someone else's, he's never been wrong about a *romance* before. Still, though—

"You should hate-fuck him about it so we don't have to talk about it anymore."

"He has a *goatee*. Pass." Oh, *God*, the goatee; Milo always forgets about that, and intentionally so.

"Well, sure." The phone rings. Milo points his scanner at Artemis. "Don't answer that."

"Ew, you think I wanna talk to customers? No." He waves a hand at the shrilling phone, and goes back to blowing his fingernails dry. "Get your skinny ass over here and do your job."

Mumbling about how his ass isn't *skinny* (it is, it's nonexistent), Milo trudges to the counter. He doesn't hop the step to get behind it, just spins the phone around to check the caller ID, and whaddaya know? It's the same guy who's already called twice today mid-wank, *evidently* because he can't take a hint. What does he think, third time's the charm and overworked, underpaid Milo is gonna listen to him come? No thanks.

This happens all the time, the semi-regulars who call to ask leading questions about lube until you realize, *Oh, this guy's jackin' it,* but it's *noon on a Tuesday,* man, c'mon. There are other hobbies. Some people just have no goddamn shame (Milo would say they have no self-respect but, believe him, these people are *plenty* proud of themselves.

(His friend and coworker Penn has fully given up and goes for the laugh: "You gotta scare 'em. Tell them your name's something threatening, like Butch. Or the Fonz.")

It is. Truly incredible. How often the store gets confused for a phone sex line, a brothel, a street corner, whatever, when this is *literally retail.* Niche retail, maybe, but *retail.*

And not that there's anything wrong with phone sex lines, brothels, street corners, whatevers. That's a whole, like, *transcendental* level of customer service that Milo can only respect. But, you know, *here* the buck stops at explaining to a parade of grown-ass adults what they should and should not shove up inside of themselves and/or others, and Milo barely gets paid enough to do *that.*

But here he is, doing *this* for the third time today, and that is… quite enough.

"Can't even be bothered to block his number." Milo gestures in the direction of below-the-counter—Artemis knows what he's after, it was his idea in the first place—just as the bell above the door ting-a-lings, announcing the arrival of an actual customer.

Shit. Well, Artemis has already handed over the air horn, and Milo is nothing if not *committed to the bit.* So he plucks up the receiver without so much as a *Hello, this is Nobody's,* and blows the air horn directly into the mouthpiece. He hears a shout, a few blistering swears, and drops the phone back into its cradle.

He tosses the air horn between his hands, whistles. "Got 'im. Fucking perv."

"That was so brave." Artemis offers him a sardonic slow-clap. "Where do I swoon?"

Milo smacks one of his boots. "Get out from behind the register, you don't *work here*."

"Troglodyte."

"I'm not going to dignify that with a response."

A laugh rings out behind him—punctuated, like she tries to stop it, but it's bright and loud and kind of infectious? It makes Milo's lips twitch. He looks over his shoulder, but she darts her eyes away, suddenly and very determinedly looking at a shelf of lubricants, hand over her mouth like she's trying not to laugh out loud again.

And she's really, *really* cute. That one hits like a sucker punch.

She's on the small side, dressed in overall shorts and a dark brown cardigan with too-long sleeves, the buttons all undone, and sneakers that have seen better days. Her dirty-blonde hair's in two braids, bobby-pinned at the sides of her head and then tied back with the rest of her hair in an artfully messy bun—the *I didn't wake up like this but I want you to wonder if I did* kind. Or, hey, maybe she did wake up like that, for all he knows.

He can't tell for sure what color her eyes are—something light, greenish-grayish?—but they're round and so is her face, her skin's sun-kissed and splashed with freckles.

She's the kind of cute that makes you say "Oh, holy shit" *out loud*—which is exactly what Milo does.

And somehow, *mercilessly*, the floor doesn't open up and swallow his dumb ass whole. Nope, it's just Belinda Carlisle on the corporate radio—fucking apropos—and Artemis's *cackle*.

"*Oh*, my Spidey senses are *tingling!*" he stage-whispers, and *gleefully*, the sicko, but at least it's a whisper as he leans across the counter to give Milo unrepentant shit. "Can't wait to talk about your emotional response to your first erection later, you *absolute* demisexual disaster."

Right. *That.* Or, well—not about the erection, Jesus, head out of the gutter! But even so, the panicked physical response sure is something. Milo's half-convinced he's gonna need to up his anxiety meds; he's even more convinced that his insurance doesn't cover *love at first sight*.

God. *Damn it.*

...and thus begins the trajectory of Milo Lamoree's indeed *absolute* crisis of sexual identity.

ROMANTICIZING THE LIFE OF A SHUT-IN

A nother day, another dick pic, another personal crisis about why she tries dating apps in the first place.

Stevie would be fascinated, probably, to know the origins of this trend no one asked for—isn't flashing a *crime*, by the way?—but she can't be bothered with anything other than her standard reply: that GIF from *Monsters, Inc.*—*put that thing back where it came from or so help meeeeee*, you know the one—and then she waits for the dude to unmatch her. Sometimes they reply, usually with an "lol" or a "????" (what further explanation *do you need*, come on, guys), and then she's the one who does the unmatching.

It's gross and unwarranted and she has to wonder if these guys have any concept of self-awareness whatsoever. She can't decide if it's worse or marginally better or really just the same as the couples trolling for a bi girl, because apparently they only exist for threesomes.

Stevie's never had a threesome. She sure as hell isn't going to go for a spin with *Jeff and Marissa, 28, happily monogamous, just looking for a girl who's down for a little bi-curious fun!* If you don't know, hey, you don't know. But Stevie, personally, isn't *curious* at all; she is *well aware*.

There's nothing fundamentally wrong with asking. She gets it! She likes sex, too. She hasn't had a ton of it or anything—she's only twenty-four and this isn't *One Tree Hill*, calm down—but it's usually a pretty good time. But when people *assume* you're down to clown because they think your sexuality is catered to their fantasies? Mmm, hard pass.

Like, *come on*—Jeff and Marissa, buy a sex doll. Not that Stevie has any psychological insight into anyone's marriage, but no way is a bi-curious tryst going to end well. That's why there are so many made-for-TV movies about it—for the *drama*—and somebody always winds up murdered. Usually the *interloper*, even though, really, it's the Jeffs who are the problem.

Either way! Stevie doesn't feel like getting murdered, thanks. She swipes left when she can, when she *knows*, but some of these people are sneaky sons of bitches. Even when it's not a surprise couple, she gets five minutes into a conversation and most guys do their way-too-interested "Soooooo have you ever been with a woman...?", and lots of women pass because "My ex-girlfriend left me for a man, so I don't really trust bi girls."

And, like. What the fuck, you know?

She likes guys and she likes girls, nonbinary, trans, *whoever's cool*. It doesn't matter! (Some people will tell you that being bi means excluding anyone who's not cis. Those people are Wrong.) If she likes you, she likes *you*. This is not a difficult concept to grasp! *And yet...*

Ugh. Whatever.

One dick pic and she's already spiraling, *God* (but it's, like, ten in the morning? Put your dick away).

Stevie heads to the kitchen, chucking her phone on the in-offensively ugly secondhand couch as she goes and aggravated Muppet-yelling all the way.

"Oh my Dolly." Tatum whacks her with the business end of the rubber spatula she's using to scramble eggs. "Don't make that noise, I am *egregiously* hungover."

She whirls the spatula with practiced gusto at the fridge, cluttered with novelty magnets and a dry-erase board that's decorated with their handwriting—Tatum's bubbly, Stevie's scribbly—in neon pinks and greens:

HOUSE RULES

1. Pop-Tarts

2. Don't forget about the spinach in the crisper, it WILL go bad!!!!!

3. Straight boys only allowed if they rinse their dishes

4. That's an oxymoron (???), so... Straight boys probably not allowed

5. Shut up, Tatum has a hangover

It would be cause for concern, maybe, but it's not like Tatum's drinking away her demons. She just has a low tolerance, always has. Stevie learned that their freshman year of college. Three wine coolers into the queer club mixer and Tatum was on the floor of the bathroom, weaving the grand tale of her life-long, tragically unreciprocated crush on Lynda Carter, before promptly throwing up. (Later she'd say she couldn't contain both alcohol *and* her feelings for Lynda Carter, which, fair; if that's not a universal human experience, *what is?*)

Stevie—who had slipped into the bathroom to get a break from all the *people*—held her hair back, and the rest, as they say, blah blah blah, is history.

Six years later, Tatum can take the harder stuff when patrons buy her shots at the gay-adjacent dive bar she works at. She'll toss a couple back for the tips, but even two or three Fireballs get to her the next day. Not quite *egregiously*, she just likes that word.

Stevie mimes zipping her lips as she rummages in the pantry for house rule #1 (the rule being, there must always be Pop-Tarts in the house—or, rather, the duplex Tatum's parents graciously let them live in for a fraction of standard rent).

"So, like, what's your problem?" Tatum asks. Stevie rips a brown sugar cinnamon in half with her teeth. "Is it because you don't put those in the toaster?"

"No, that's *your* problem."

"They're called *Pop*-Tarts, not Raw-Dog-It-Tarts."

Undeterred, Stevie shoves the other half in her mouth. "That is... *not* what that means."

"Mm. They're both equally upsetting."

"What do you know about *raw dogging*, you're a lesbian."

"A-*ha*!" Tatum points the spatula at her. "That means I know everything."

"So *you* tell me what my problem is. Asshole."

"Hm." Tatum sprinkles a too-generous helping of pepper into her eggs and flips them in the skillet. "You're a freaky little gremlin person who needs a better conditioner. Seriously, you look like you've been electrocuted."

Uncalled for. First of all, not everyone can be blessed with Tatum O'Leary's no-muss, no-fuss curtain of perfectly dark red locks (and it's comments like this that make Stevie regret holding her hair back in the first place). Between that and her *green*-green eyes and general willowy-ness, she looks like a mermaid. It's obnoxious.

Meanwhile, *some of them* have to get a decent color out of a box—just some platinum highlights, something that pops, to liven up her otherwise dishwater-blonde, uncontrollable sort-of-but-not-quite curls that are even less manageable when cut short, so they tumble halfway down her back in the rare moments she doesn't have a scrunchie on hand.

Second of all, Stevie just woke up, of course it looks bad.

"*Asshole,*" she says again. She weaves her hair into a quick braid, tied off with a rubber band from the junk drawer.

"Oh, don't give me those baby cow eyes." Tatum dumps her eggs between two pieces of toast and talks around a huge bite. "What'd you do, check your Tinder right when you woke up? Bad start to the day, my man."

"Yeah, I've already had a whole meltdown about it," Stevie admits. She pours instant coffee and cocoa powder into a shaker cup. "Now I can get on with my day."

"The best part of waking up, is an emotional breakdown in your cup," Tatum sing-songs. With a full mouth, mind you. "This is what happens when you only socialize with your phone. When was the last time you left the house? You should come out to Loretta's this week."

Stevie shrugs—her usual answer. And, to her credit, Tatum (mostly) accepts.

"Alright." She hums. "Well, let me know, okay? I'm not totally sure who's coming in tonight, but Dottie texted me earlier, she said she's swinging by tomorrow."

Oh, well, in that case Stevie probably will go. She just doesn't like to commit to anything, in case her future self is shocked and appalled by the notion of *plans*.

Speaking of! She digs out the Paxil from behind the pink Himalayan salt—yeah, yeah, maybe the spice cupboard isn't *the place* to store her meds, *shush*—and pops her prescribed 20mg, washed down with a swig of hot chocolate coffee that's grainy as all hell, she didn't shake it well enough. Breakfast of champions.

"Stop. Please. I can't watch you eat that shit for breakfast again." Tatum grabs a mug—the one with the dandelion and its dead-eyed, dainty smile, emblazoned with *Blow Me*—out of the cabinet and pours her a fresh coffee, topped off with a generous serving of white chocolate syrup. She hands off the rest of her scrambled egg sandwich, too. "Just, *something* reasonable, please."

Well, Stevie's not going to say no to a better breakfast; she just doesn't like to cook. Maybe it makes her feel a little bit like a toddler, when Tatum has to regulate her diet, but then again Stevie's the one who doesn't mind cleaning the shower drain, so, it all balances out.

While Tatum tidies up the kitchen, Stevie gets settled at the living room coffee table for work, criss-cross-applesauce on the floor, back braced against the couch. She powers on her heavily-stickered laptop, hits shuffle on Spotify, and flips through her planner to check this week's to-do list.

Between her social anxiety and agoraphobia (which aren't the same thing, but honestly she has trouble differentiating, they overlap enough), Stevie secured government assistance. It took two years and so much paperwork that she does in fact feel personally responsible for some sort of environmental depletion.

She gets by with or without regular work, but she likes to supplement her checks with graphic designer gigs. Call it an ego thing, or a not-that-irrational fear that the government will eventually stop helping her and instead hunt her for sport, either way Stevie needs to keep herself busy.

She does some contract work and she's got a pretty steady backlog of personal clients, mostly indie authors, that she sort of lucked into. She worked for it, sure, but hard work paying off is still a stroke of luck with things like this. It's all about hashtags and timing and who you know, rather than actual talent and skill. Equal parts discouraging and liberating—it's very much like, nothing matters, so just do whatever you want. Gig work is, if nothing else, *thrilling* (and Stevie says that only a tad sarcastically).

There are a couple things on the docket she can get done today, so long as Photoshop doesn't have one of its sudden and inexplicable vendettas against her. She's just gotta *believe*, man.

Fingers crossed while she boots up the program, Tatum appears in the doorway and offers her a sign of the cross in solidarity. Technically meaningless, since both of their religious sensibilities begin and end with *somebody better have my back, because I'm about to wing it*. But the thought's appreciated.

"I'm going back to bed," Tatum announces, "until three P.M. Car keys are on that ugly fish plate from Goodwill if you feel like being a well-adjusted human person."

"I guess I could go for a McChicken."

"That's the least well-adjusted thing you've ever said."

Oh-ho-ho, *far* from it. But before Stevie can argue this point for no apparent reason, Tatum keeps talking.

"One more thing! I'm thinking, and I am *just saying*," she *just says* from her bedroom doorway. "Maybe instead of wasting your time on swiping, you should practice a little *self-love*, if you know what I mean."

Stevie blinks at her, just once. "I do. I do know what you mean. That wasn't subtle."

"*Well...*" Tatum starts thrusting, keeping up a rhythm as she walks backwards into her room, like some kind of overtly sexual rendition of the Running Man.

"Even less subtle now!"

"Not one of my strong suits, anyway!" And with that, Tatum's bedroom door swings shut with no small amount of flair.

Aurgh. One minute it's unsolicited dick pics, the next your best friend's telling you to masturbate more often. Stevie's starting to wish she had the emotional constitution to go fully celibate.

She tries—no dice, though—to ignore the other thing Tatum said, about *wasting her time*. Because that's the real kick in the pants, isn't it, is that nothing ever works out. *Trying* feels like a fool's errand.

Not to be totally macabre about it or anything, she's just tired of feeling stupid over people who aren't worth it. Maybe it's not even the people she feels stupid about, it's more her own desperate hope that *this time will be different.*

It's never different. Sometimes it's never anything at all.

Oh, God, here she is, indulging in full-on *ennui* about the state of her love life—and love in general, even!—and her playlist kicks up with "I Just Had Sex" by the Lonely Island.

It's comedic timing like this that makes Stevie think maybe she really is living in a romantic comedy—barring the fact that, best case scenario, dating is an awkward series of fizzled-out conversations with Tinder matches. Not exactly feel-good script material.

She switches over to her *an attempt to romanticize my boring life* playlist; if she's going to bemoan the very concept of love, she's going to do it soundtracked by Hootie & the Blowfish. For the *atmosphere.*

To the tune of "Only Wanna Be With You," Stevie crumples to the floor between the coffee table and the couch, groaning as she goes.

Much as she doesn't want to think about what Tatum said, because it *bums her out*, maybe she doesn't have to think about it in its entirety, you know? If the big picture's too much to take first thing in the morning, well, she can take it step by step.

So, bearing that in mind...

Alright. Maybe she does just need to get off and then she'll be normal again. Sure, it always works better for her when it's with someone else, because she likes the *kissing*, and the *touching*, and the shivery anticipation before Something Happens, but, needs must. Sometimes an orgasm's just a means to an end, right? It's like forcing yourself to wash your hair and clean your room—it's self-care, a refresher, a reminder that, oh, maybe life's not complete and total hell, you were just hungry.

Stevie gropes for her phone, still on the couch, and looks up the hours for Nobody's Secret. The greatest invention known to man, she thinks, is the "popular times" feature, so she can figure out whether or not to go somewhere. Nobody's is dead around noon, so noon it is.

See, she's perfectly capable of managing her agoraphobia, even if she hasn't left the house in eight days.

(Okay, yeah, so she's a disaster. What else is new?)

Huffing a disgruntled kind of noise, Stevie swipes her screen and opens Tinder. To *delete it*. Not *once and for all* or anything, no, she's done this too many times to have any faith in herself whatsoever, but *for right now* will have to do the trick.

What *trick* remains to be seen. Or, not seen, because let's be real—appropriate soundtrack notwithstanding—her life isn't a romantic comedy. It just... is what it is, and the romantic possibilities therein have been forgettable at best.

And the *effort*! Ugh. The effort is tiresome, fruitless, and whatever other disheartening adjective you can think of. So, sure, if she wants a little affection, maybe self-love is the best she'll ever do.

And even if Stevie Hart's self-esteem at present isn't *quite* equipped for loving herself unconditionally (*oof*, but—), that is *her business*.

It's probably nothing a good vibrator can't fix, anyway.

MEET-CUTES AND QUESTIONABLE LUBRICANTS

T his is so stupid. So so so so so stupid.

The whole bright side of being demisexual is that you don't have to deal with your brain short-circuiting over *cute*. Of course, the drawback is that nobody seems to know what demisexuality is—read: your sexual attraction/feelings aren't based on physicality, but rather on an emotional connection. But on the occasions that Milo's disclosed what his deal is, the responses don't go much beyond "Isn't that how it is for everybody?" (oh-ho-ho *no*) and "But what are you *really*?" (he's not entirely sure what this means).

And really, all that's a best-case scenario. Milo's long since packed up the worst-case scenario bullshit he's dealt with, shoved it to the back of his mind where it will surely and inevitably develop into an ulcer. Maybe he already has the ulcer, *who knows.*

But despite the drawbacks, despite all the bullshit, Milo's supposed to be able to live *peacefully*, unhindered by *lascivious distraction*, and yet *here he is*, in the middle of a goddamn workday, no less, rendered utterly and completely useless over the scattered beauty marks up the side of some girl's thigh, or—or—*whatever* this is, but his brain has indeed well and truly short-circuited, so he hardly even knows.

Nope! All he knows, in fact, is that *pretty girl pretty girl pretty girl* is doing laps around his brain like some kind of sadistic sexuality merry-go-round. Like, is this a soulmate thing (so he's a romantic, sue him), or is this just how people feel when they figure out they're attracted to girls? He resolves to ask one of the bartenders at Loretta's. They're all lesbians, surely they've got some insight.

(Milo also knows plenty of straight men, but he'd bet his next paycheck none of them would be as eloquent about it. They usually say something about a girl's tits and that explains every-thing? Meanwhile every wlw in Milo's acquaintance has a sense of *romance* about these things; "I'd let her hit me with a Mack truck" seems to be the universal measurement of attraction. It's got a certain *panache*, you know?)

It's not that Milo's never seen a good-looking person before, hello, he does go out in public. He *has* dated before (sort of? Though he called that quits about three years ago now), but he doesn't have a *type*. That's not how this works. Artemis just has this, like, sixth sense—talk about quitting their jobs, seriously, he could make bank in matchmaking. Milo's seen him do it before, but he's never been on the receiving end. And now that he is, well, he fucking hates it, man.

Because Artemis is *glowing* with the aura of sick smug sat-isfaction and Milo *thinks* this is what schadenfreude is and he really, really doesn't feel like deep-diving into sociological concepts right now, but then again maybe that's preferable to whatever's happening to him?

Which, if pressed, Milo would boil it down to an existential crisis. It feels *big* and kind of terrible and it's completely warped his sense of self and, indeed, his sense of reality as a whole.

(*Yes*, he's prone to dramatics, why do you ask? He grew up on early 2000s romcoms, these things are *formative*.)

Milo leans over the counter, *slumped*, *defeated*, and with all the machismo in the world (*ha!*), he begs, "I will give you a thousand dollars to *please leave*."

Artemis places a hand against his chest. "There is, sincerely, from the bottom of my heart, no way that you have a thousand dollars."

"...Twelve dollars."

"Hm. Venmo me." Artemis stands, whipping his tastefully sequined bomber jacket over his shoulders. "Or I'll be back."

Milo waves him off with one hand, while the other taps the transaction into his phone. They do this all the time; that twelve dollars has been in limbo for *years* with no end in sight. At this point it's less about the money and more about the bit.

Once Artemis is out of the immediate vicinity of ruining his life, Milo switches to customer service mode. It's usually easy, second nature, but now he's contending with at least three different crises (personal, sexual, existential), so, jury's out, he'll see how this goes. Nervous habit, he cracks his knuckles. He steps on the creaky spot in the floor, too, in case this girl's too absorbed in the price comparison of lubricants to notice him.

She has a tattoo of a fat, cartoonish ladybug that looks kinda like the Beanie Baby crawling its way around her wrist, and it directs Milo to the box in her hand. It's the generic stuff you can buy anywhere, *prominently* including your local gas station. Which. Oof. Bad choice. He's got a civic duty to stop this immediately.

"Ah—" He plucks the box from her hand, tosses it and catches it in his own. "Don't buy that."

She blinks at him (her eyes *are* greenish-grayish, point to Milo). "Oh. Um. Why not?"

"One of the main ingredients is sugar, basically. Save yourself the yeast infection."

Underpaid as he is, one perk of this job is that you can pretty much say whatever you want. *For instance*, there's no other way to say "cock ring," so, defer to your own judgment all you want, but a spade's a spade, baby, everybody knows what they're here for. And Milo does actually care about the health and well-being of Nobody's customers. There's something decidedly psychotic, or at least *malicious*, about a sex shop rep who doesn't.

His altruistic motives seem to be lost on this customer, though, because the next thing she asks is, "Can you say that?"

"Can I—" Milo blinks at her right back, caught somewhere between insulted and a laugh. "What do you mean, *can I say that*? It's on the box. See—"

He flips the box in question and taps the side. "Glycerin. It breaks down into sugar. I'm not saying a yeast infection's inevitable, and the heated stuff here"—he indicates the bottom shelf, because that's where they keep the generic brands—"is actually super nice for, like, back massages, whatever, but, uh. Not exactly your best option for internal use. We stock it because people expect us to, and they buy it 'cause it's cheap, but if it messes with your pH balance, I mean, you're paying more for antibiotics than you would on a higher-quality lube. Might as well cut out the middleman."

Another blink. Which, sure, that's a lot of information he just hit her with. "The middleman being a—yeast infection?"

"Ah. Yes."

"Right." She dips into her slouchy shoulder bag and comes out with a... Rubik's cube? Milo declines to comment as she fidgets with it. "Well. Yeah, I'm definitely not interested in, y'know. *That.* So. Okay. Would you mind pointing me to something less, um. Infectious?"

"God, yes, you'd be doing my blood pressure a favor." Milo grins, genuinely relieved. She laughs again; he wants to eat it. (And, Christ, what is *that* about??)

He points out the options, suggests water-based—"A silicone base is bad news bears for silicone toys, which sounds wrong, you'd think they'd go together but they just, uh, *do not*, so unless you're using your toys in the shower like all the time, I'd stick with the water, or a hybrid's okay, too"—and flavored—"If you're into that, but I swear to God they could sell the mocha stuff at, like, Dunkin' and pass it off as real coffee"—and she's more at ease the more he rambles on and on.

That's not unusual. Most women who come in prefer to talk to another woman, and unless Penn—who's nonbinary, but has more of a girly aesthetic—is on the schedule, it takes a bit for them to be comfortable with Milo, if they get comfortable at all. He gets it, he does, but it's a bummer when he can't help someone out. He really, honestly, *pure of heart*, just wants people to be safe and smart about what they're doing.

Sure, he loses his patience with Erik and the dudes like him who are in and out of the store, but they're just so *brazen* about how willfully ignorant they are. The girls tend to be more shy and embarrassed and a lot of other things the midwestern school system taught them to be.

Milo can't fault them for that. It's one thing to think you can stick an anal vibrator wherever you want, and a whole other one to unlearn the shame spiral you've been forced into since fifth-grade sex ed.

This girl warms up to him pretty quick. Seems to, anyway, and Milo's pretty good at reading people; you have to be in this line of work. You don't want to say too much or make the wrong joke to the wrong person, because that doesn't go over too hot. But jokes make some people feel at ease, so it's all about testing the waters *tactfully*.

She doesn't make eye contact but her shoulders relax, and she never mumbles anything about how *embarrassing* this is. So, not a bad start. He doesn't get what the Rubik's cube's about, but he lets her fidget and he holds on to the stuff they pick out. Because they don't quit at lube, no, she asks him about toy cleaner, too.

"So is soap and water not as okay as I thought it was?"

Milo flinches. "Oh—*no*. No, uh. Soap wears down the plastic, so your toys don't last as long. And if it's a silicone toy, well, so—silicone is porous, so think about it the same way you think about your face. Most people use specific face wash that's made for pores, because all soap does is clog those up. And if they're clogged, they don't get clean. And if they don't get clean, they grow bacteria. And then, y'know, in the case of sex toys"—he clicks his tongue, jerks his thumb—"we're back to the yeast infection."

"Gosh." She raises her eyebrows at the shelf in front of them. "Jeez. It's just. It's always a yeast infection, huh?"

"Yeah, it's—ha." He snorts. "That's why people think silicone toys are lousy, but really it's because they're being unhygienic about it. Soap and water's alright for glass toys, those clean as easy as a casserole dish, but otherwise..."

He plucks a bottle of toy cleaner from the shelf, wiggles it. "Have I sold you, or should I zip it?"

She swipes her hands, one palm out and the other still curled around her Rubik's, in front of her. "Sold. My health insurance is just okay."

Milo whistles. "I feel that. And thank you, genuinely, I am..." He trails off for a second to laugh. "*Endlessly* worried about, like, eighty-six percent of the people who shop here."

She laughs, too, this short huff of breath through her pierced nose. "And here I was, almost another statistic."

Well, when it comes to the *narrow* breadth of Milo's capacity for sexual attraction, she's definitely an outlier. That, or! He has the sudden and very reasonable (read: not reasonable at all) thought that maybe he's bad at being demisexual. As if someone's grading him on his sexuality—which, actually, big reason why he avoids social media—like he's got a membership card that can be taken away as soon as he doesn't fit tidily into his designated box.

He needs to chill the fuck out.

She mentions needing a new vibrator—"My old one is... Well. I get what you're saying about the toy cleaner now"—so Milo leaves her alone at the wall, lets her know he's around if she has any questions. He's filled her in on the things people don't tend to know, now he doesn't want to hover. Working here, you walk a fine line between 'helpful customer service' and 'nosey lech who should be fired and also punched in the dick.'

He starts breaking down the inventory boxes he's emptied. His phone is on a shelf below the register, the cracked screen lighting up every minute or so with new texts and reminders that he hasn't checked them yet. Nor does he *want to*, mind. No doubt it's his friends having a field day over whatever Artemis must have told them in the half-hour he's been gone. *I don't want to know I don't want to know I do not want to know—*

Alright, so maybe he wants to know a little bit. What can he say, he has no impulse control.

Milo's just swiped the screen when the inadvertent upender of his world is ready to check out, and he once again shifts seamlessly into his customer service persona.

"Sorry." He tosses his phone, sends it clattering across the counter and onto the floor. Milo blinks at it. Okay, so much for *seamlessly.* "Uh. All set?"

"Mhm." She glances over to where his phone disappeared, pressing her lips together against a smile, and sets down her items. A second passes before she realizes she left her Rubik's cube there, too; she mumbles her own apology and tucks the toy into her bag.

It's *almost* an opening to ask her what that's about, but the mumbling stops him from doing so. Also she's a customer, he doesn't even know her, et cetera, et cetera, the list goes on. It seems like a weird thing, sure, but you don't just ask people about their weird things unless you want to make them *feel* weird about it.

He rings her out, checks her ID against her debit card—not for creep reasons, he legitimately has to ask, and if he happens to remember that her name is Stevie for the rest of his sorry life, well, *fine*—and he's entirely chill and normal the whole time. Forget what his probably-even-more-cracked-now phone would try to tell you otherwise.

"Thanks for all your help," she says, collecting the crinkly bag and stowing that away in her purse, too. She adjusts the strap a bit tighter. "So, um. Have a good rest of your day?"

Milo clicks his tongue against the roof of his mouth, drums his fingers on the countertop. "Think that's my line." He smiles when she does. "You, too."

"Thanks," Stevie says again, and she's off, nothing but a sheepish smile over her shoulder when the door gets caught on the floor mat. She unsticks it and the bell trips over its ting-a-ling, and then she's gone.

God.

What. A. *Day*. Milo releases a long, slow breath that does nothing for the nervous tangle of his heartbeat.

Overcome with the sudden urge to move, to *do* something, he shakes his head, ruffles his curls, and snatches his phone off the floor. No new cracks, after all—a miracle heretofore unbeknownst to man—and unlocks the screen.

***

ARTEMIS: Ladies and theydies, I have an ANNOUNCEMENT

DOTTIE: And some of us have JOBS.

ARTEMIS: Excuse me? I'm basically Milo's sugar daddy
SOME OF US just take vacations

DOTTIE: Relax. I'm not busy, I don't have another patient until three.

ARTEMIS: ME relax???

DOTTIE: Shush. All I do all day is talk about feelings, I don't have time for yours.

ARTEMIS: Fair.

PENN: ...is it safe to come out?

ARTEMIS: You're such a wimp

PENN: i don't like confrontation!!!

ARTEMIS: You work in CUSTOMER SERVICE

PENN: you know what?
point to you.
what's the announcement?

ARTEMIS: Milo has a CRUSH

PENN: ooooh. diiiiiiiish, please.

ARTEMIS: That's it, that's the dish
She came into the store, Milo had a mild but totally survivable heart attack (drama queen), and then he kicked me out

ARTEMIS: OH, and this all happened over the course of "Heaven Is A Place On Earth." Which seminal teen movie are we living in, do you think??

PENN: see!! THERE'S the dish!

PENN: @ dottie, what's the diagnosis, doctor??

DOTTIE: That depends. Just tell me it's not Whitney this time.

ARTEMIS: *hisses* NO, thank the deity of your choice

PENN: //phew// blech, gross, gag me

MILO: *typing...*

DOTTIE: Oh, here he goes.

MILO: FIRST OF ALL

ARTEMIS: Ugh.

MILO: would it kill you ppl to mind ur own business!!!

ARTEMIS: Staying out of your friends' business is a straight people thing. They're too busy shopping for cargo shorts and coming up with increasingly nonsense spellings for Amy/Aimee/Aimy/Eymee.

PENN: i think that last one's a pokémon.

DOTTIE: Interesting thesis. (Not about the Pokémon, that's just plain correct.)

ARTEMIS: Are you refuting it?

DOTTIE: I'm a therapist, not a professor. Live your bliss.

PENN: put that on your business cards

MILO: SECOND OF ALL

ARTEMIS: Ew, are you still here?

MILO: whatever's wrong with me rn does not constitute an ANNOUNCEMENT

DOTTIE: "Whatever's wrong with me rn" in regards to a ~crush~ might be the most demisexual thing you've ever said.

MILO: a-HA! u are conveniently forgetting that one time i drunkenly declared that my sexual preference is "we'll see how it goes"

ARTEMIS: The *one* time

PENN: /one/ and /eighteen billion/ are synonyms, didn't u know?

MILO: *typing...*

MILO: *typing...*

ARTEMIS: Quick, someone punch the game show buzzer

MILO: forget it!!!!!!

MILO: YOU'RE ALL SHUNNED

***

TATUM: I see my car's gone, does that mean you took my advice?

STEVIE: that makes it sound like your advice was that i should masturbate in your car

TATUM: I mean, a little exhibitionism might loosen you up? But also DON'T, I just vacuumed it

STEVIE: well in that case what i'm doing rn might be worse

TATUM: Diiiiiid yoooooouuuuuu......

TATUM: Murder someone?

STEVIE: no, i'm eating my feelings in the taco bell parking lot

TATUM: ??? Eating your feelings in the Taco Bell parking lot is strictly 'Mom called me' Stevie behavior.
What does Rachel want NOW?

STEVIE: hey
my feelings are wide and varied
MULTIFACETED

TATUM: Yeah, yeah, I know, it takes you approx 5-8 business days to process, I'll give you -space-

STEVIE: it's not my mom, tho. so nothing immediately dire.

TATUM: Will be absolutely fascinated to hear what else gets you chowing down on half a dozen bacon club Chalupas in broad daylight to the tune of "The Tracks of My Tears" played so loud that you're probably going to need to replace my speakers

TATUM: There's just no way that's -never- going to happen, I can feel it in my bones

STEVIE: *typing...*

STEVIE: *typing...*

STEVIE: you know too much abt me

TATUM: That song is so specifically about a breakup, -why- is it your go-to for every emotional problem you have??

STEVIE: if u can't belt out all your repressed feelings to that chorus, then idk how u cope with the abject horrors of being alive

TATUM: You know me, nothing does it like Britney

STEVIE: fair and valid.

TATUM: I'll let you get back to it, we'll deep-dive into it later. Pick me up a Doritos Locos combo?

STEVIE: obviously

TATUM: Bless your emotionally unstable heart x

SICK OF DATING APPS, JUST GONNA PYGMALION MYSELF A BOYFRIEND

L oretta's isn't overly crowded at eight P.M., so Stevie takes her usual seat at the corner of the bar and plans to stay *there* until she's ready to call it a night.

Owned by a lesbian couple so business-savvy that they're always on vacation, Loretta's is less what you'd expect of a gay bar, more of your regular small-town dive, albeit with more of a queer attitude. Everyone is welcome, no side-eyes about it unless you're the one side-eyeing the regulars or the décor.

The walls are plastered with every iteration of Pride flag, old and new, and framed posters, headshots, selfies of queer icons: Marsha P. Johnson and Sylvia Rivera, Gilbert Baker, Lady Phyll, Freddie Mercury and Judy Garland and Jennifer Coolidge, Chaz Bono and Sylvester and Hannah Gadsby and Big Freedia, Lena Waithe and BD Wong and Marco from *Degrassi* (Adamo Ruggiero! Stevie can never remember all the Degrassi kids off the cuff, but there you go), the *Queer Eye* crew and the cast of *The Gay and Wondrous Life of Caleb Gallo*, Tinky Winky and the Babadook...

They run the gamut, clearly, and it goes on. Stevie's got her reservations about that last one, but she'll give it to him—the dude looks good in a feather boa.

There are newspaper clippings and handmade signs, too, from decades of protests and movements—the Stonewall riots, the AIDS crisis, marriage equality and pro-choice and trans rights. Polaroids, faded banners, and other mementos from Pride celebrations are on display behind the bar, along with such a heavily graffitied poster of Ronald Reagan that you can hardly see his face anymore. Good riddance.

On the whole, Loretta's is a veritable collection of all the good, bad, and ugly that's woven into queer history. But then, even so, it is still a bar with sticky floors and ambient lighting (that is to say, there's a funny purple-blue tint to everything and nobody can fucking see).

Talk about the *duality of man.*

The music is kept at a reasonable volume so you can actually hear what the people you're with are saying. They only blast the sound for one song at a time, and only under very specific circumstances:

- "9 to 5" by Dolly Parton, obviously, and especially around six on Friday nights

- Alex Newell's "Attitude," when one of the regulars is going through a slump, and everyone else thinks it's high time they start feeling themselves again

- "I Wanna Dance With Somebody," again, *obviously*—no stipulations, just vibes

- At eleven, give or take, when everyone's juuuuuust tipsy enough to Feel Good and they want to sing along to "Sweet Caroline" (*bah-bah-baaaaah*)

- "Faith," when everyone's a little more than juuuuuust tipsy enough

- And "Closing Time," because last call was a goddamn hour ago and it's time to clear out, *for the love of God*

Stevie's heard the first few plenty, but she's never around for that last one (she only has Tatum's exasperation for reference), and very seldom is she around for the one or two before that. The crowd filters in between nine and ten, and it's usually more than she's comfortable with, so, sayonara and all that. She's back home with Chinese takeout and an SVU marathon (what do you want from her, okay, Mariska Hargitay is *everyone on the planet's* siren call) in record time.

But right now, it's just a smidge past eight on Weekend Wednesday, when drinks are half-off and everyone's wearing tie-dye for reasons no one remembers anymore. The rush isn't due for another hour or so. Stevie can still breathe just fine, and trying to decide whether she prefers Benson and Stabler or Benson and Cabot or Benson and Barba can wait. (But, see, it's Benson and *everyone*. Hargitay, man. She's got the range.)

Tatum tried to coax her out last night, but Stevie had passed after the whole... *thing*, at Nobody's. Not that it was *a thing*, per se, no capital T required, she was totally fine and very normal about it, thanks.

Just. Well. It's kind of annoying, actually?

Is dating really so harsh that some guy caring about her pH balance is the great and unmitigated romance the likes of which not even *While You Were Sleeping* has ever seen? Like, the snow globe was nice, Bill Pullman, but these days the threshold for grand romantic gestures is an applicable knowledge of the ingredients in popularized lubricants, otherwise you can just *forget it.*

Annoying as it may be, the dick pics and intense biphobia that dominate her inbox considered, how annoyed can she be? The guy was just doing his job. If Stevie's all *titillated* about it, that's her own problem.

And maybe it's not even a problem! Maybe *cares about your pH balance* should be as low as the bar goes. Stevie knows more than one married couple who don't discuss gynecology appointments for reasons unbeknownst to the realms of logical thinking, so—if this is her new standard, so be it.

She just wishes she could separate the standard from the person, you know?

But, gosh, he'd been cute. Tall, a little broad and a little lanky, and his left eye had veered a little crooked (and maybe she'd Googled that when she got home, not because it bothered her, she's not an asshole, but just because she wanted to know). He had a big smile and a spray of freckles with no rhyme or reason across his face, wild curls that his scrunchie—his *scrunchie!*—did almost absolutely nothing for.

And he'd been so *nice,* easy to talk to, and that's the part that gets her, because Stevie doesn't have an easy time talking to just anybody.

But that's his *job.* The last thing Stevie needs is to go projecting her fantasies onto some poor unsuspecting retail rep. Best case scenario, she'll end up woefully disappointed. Story of her life, no matter how badly she wants to rewrite it.

It's... surreal, sometimes, to juggle disillusionment and hope at the same time? But! *Again*—that's her problem.

Carly Rae Jepsen starts playing on the speakers and Tatum slides her a glass of vodka lemonade. It's like she can smell the existential crisis—which, maybe that's just a bartender thing?

Also a sex therapist thing, surely, because just then Dottie says, like she's never seen anything more hilarious, "What is wrong with you?"

"Does something seem like it's wrong with me? Actually. Wait." Stevie grimaces around her paper straw. "I don't know if I want you to answer that."

This only makes Dottie laugh. Which would be worrisome, offensive, *something*, but Dottie's got a great laugh. A powerful laugh, even, it really lulls you into a false sense of security. Stevie's known Dottie long enough to know better, though.

Dr. Dottie Carmichael, of indeterminate age because "Excuse me? That's none of your business" (she's forty-two, she just wants to pull the ageless-possibly-immortal angle, like Keanu Reeves), is simultaneously the kindest and most intimidating person Stevie's ever met. Go figure; that's what you get by being hot and having a PhD.

Dottie favors glittery eyeshadow, bright matte lipstick, and comfortable shoes. She wears her ombre-dyed hair in a blunt cut that stops just above her shoulders, but even so she's perfected the expert hair-flip whenever the situation calls for it. She's five-foot-five but all the same an *imposing* fixture at Loretta's. She lives in the city about half an hour away, but she comes to town every couple of weeks for dinner with her grandma and then drinks out with her friends. Sometimes her husband comes, too, but mostly he respects her need for uninhibited friendship time.

When they're out on the town, Dottie's tab is comped by any- and everyone who hounds her for advice about their sex lives. Dottie doesn't mind—anything for a continuous rotation of tequila sunrises, right? And she's always said that being a Black trans woman means she doesn't have time to entertain anybody's bullshit, so it only takes her about ten minutes, tops, to cut to the heart of everyone's latest problem.

Stevie wants to be her when she grows up. Big dreams, since Stevie mostly feels entirely bogged down by her own neuroses. Meh. What're you gonna do?

"I could ask you how you're doing," Dottie says, "but nobody ever tells the truth about that."

"So, what, asking what's wrong with me is...?"

"A foregone conclusion." She tugs affectionately at the pastel tie-dye scarf in Stevie's hair. "Something's definitely wrong with you."

She says it so matter-of-fact, it's not even insulting. It just is what it is. God damn it, no wonder Dottie's so good at her job.

"*Aurgh*," Stevie groans a halfhearted Charlie Brown impression, flicks aside her straw and tosses back a gulp of her drink. "I'm sick of everyone knowing all my innermost secrets. I want to be *aloof*."

"Ha! No, you don't. You know who's aloof? Whitney," Dottie answers herself. "And nobody likes goddamn Whitney."

Well, that's both true and not. People tolerate Whitney or they wind up dating her or, in Tatum's case, it's back and forth, back and forth, drama drama drama. So when you put it that way, it all sounds exhausting and, okay, maybe Stevie doesn't want to be like that even a little bit.

Dottie waves at someone across the bar. Stevie turns and waves, too, when she sees Madison, pretty and perky and their token straight friend, with a few equally pretty and perky and (maybe, maybe not, it's their own personal business) straight coworkers from the local salon and spa.

"Thank God she didn't bring a date this time," Dottie says. "She's got the worst taste in men. You know I hear she's been seeing Erik?"

Ugh. Stevie goes back to her drink. "I do *not* want to hear about who's dating Erik."

Dottie hums. "Next thing you know she's gonna start bringing him here. *Oh*, yeah," she goes on while Stevie groans, "he's gonna show up and queue up the jukebox with *Hoobastank* for two hours straight. Can you imagine?"

"You're forcing me to."

"Please, I don't even think they have any Hoobastank. That's just sad white boy jerk-off music, isn't it? So not appropriate for a public venue, mm mm mm." Dottie shakes her head. "Speaking of dating, that's what's wrong with you, isn't it? You don't want to talk about what Erik's doing, fine, I can switch focus. So what's going on with you?"

"Tinder."

"Oh, peach, you gotta set up a serious appointment with me." Stevie snorts. "I couldn't afford you."

"Mm, too true. Well, your unintentional hilarity is charming, so, gratis"—Dottie snaps her fingers, bops her on the nose—"get off that app."

Another groan, muffled when Stevie blows bubbles into her vodka lemonade. "How am I supposed to meet people?"

"*Have* you met anyone? Exactly," Dottie says, again without waiting for an answer because it's not like she needs one. "I'm not saying it doesn't work for some people, but it's not gonna work for you."

Stevie props her chin in her hand, raises an eyebrow. "Because I'm an acquired taste?"

"Maybe a little." Another peal of laughter. "*Because*, peach, it just puts you in such a mood. And not any of the good ones."

"Yeah, well." Stevie waves her off. "I already deleted it again, anyway. Let's see how drunk I get tonight, though, I'll have that sucker downloaded all over again. Thirty-eighth time's the charm," she adds dully.

"I wouldn't be surprised if that was your real number."

She'd lost count somewhere between twelve and thirteen, so it's hard to say, but thirty-eight's not too bad a bet.

Dottie is, as per ush, soon enough called away on business. Not hard to see that one coming, since the table behind them had been having an increasingly loud conversation about the psychology behind monster-fucking ("*Lordt*, we might have found the one thing I'm not prepared for"), and Stevie is left to her own devices. She could follow Dottie, but she's been babysat enough and it's not, like, the *beeeest* feeling? So.

She scrolls on her phone, refreshing social feeds to no avail, before giving up and going for her Rubik's cube. Tatum replaces her drink, gives her a quick *Everything okay?* look, to which Stevie twirls a noncommittal hand; she'll be fine.

The thing about *fine*, though, is that it's full of shit—like how whenever someone says they're fine, that's just a bald-faced *lie*—so there must be some divine intervention going on here, when Stevie remotely suggests she'll be fine, and ten seconds later she's not fine at all.

Because ten seconds later, the unofficial but apparent spokesman for vaginal hygiene slides right on up to the bar.

Literally slides, by the way, backtracked by more Carly Rae Jepsen as his sneakers squeak across the sparkly tiled floor. He catches the edge of the bar top and braces his hands against it, hoists himself up a bit taller and whistles in Tatum's direction like he's calling for an untrained puppy.

Tatum flips him off. "Keep it up, Milo, I'll charge you full price."

"I have an important question!" he insists. "About *lesbianism*."

That gets him nothing but an eye-roll before Tatum goes back to ignoring him. Milo deflates like a punctured bounce house, forlorn whistle and all. Stevie can't help a laugh, and the sound catches his attention just like it did yesterday at the store.

When Milo turns to look at her, maybe Stevie's imagining it, but he perks up (right? Right).

"Oh, no way." A grin flashes across his face. "Hey."

"Hi." Amazing that she can speak at all with the butterflies swarming her throat.

Ahem. Stevie twists the Rubik's cube with more force than she needs to, spinning the top row like she's trying to open a stubborn jar.

She's *fine*, this is fine—

Except why does he have to *look* like that?

His—*Milo's*, the name suits him—jeans and T-shirt sleeves are cuffed; he's got a tie-dye headband in his hair, too, although the colors are brighter than Stevie's and it makes his curls stick up at every angle. There's a tattoo on his upper arm, one she hadn't noticed yesterday thanks to his flannel button-down. It's a half-sleeve cascade of falling leaves and flowers she can't name, and a quote she can't make out is scribbled along the inside of his arm. The whole thing is bold black lines and shadows, no pop of color to be found.

It's all so *endearing*. Charming and cute, a suggestion of *weird* around the edges. She wants to be his best friend. She wants to kiss him on the mouth. And she wants to kick herself in the shin, because you can't get more *projecting your fantasies* than all *that*.

Milo's giving her his own once-over—more curious than *thirsty*, but still! So if she's going full parasocial infatuation with her local retailer, maybe he's reciprocating?

"So," he says, smiling like he was made to smile at her, "now you know, I'm Milo. And you are either mysterious customer who will remain an enigma if she feels like it, no further questions asked, oooor...?"

"The girl who gave you her ID yesterday," Stevie reminds him. "Or did you just pretend to check it against my debit card?"

A surprised *ha!* escapes his grin. "*Damn it.* Fine, so I know your name's Stevie, I just didn't want to be a creep about it."

"That's very noble."

"Is that all it takes?" Milo whistles. "Oof, the bar is *low*."

Sure is. Hadn't Stevie just been thinking the same thing? And here Milo is, showing up out of the blue and all self-aware. Bah. Of course she's practically in love with him already.

There is either something deeply wrong with her, or maybe this is all because she didn't bother to masturbate in the day and a half since she decided that must be her problem.

No, she let the problem *fester*, and now here she is, deeply wrong with no idea what to do about it. In *public*.

Fucking. *Cripes*.

Milo's gaze drops to her fidgeting hands. He plants his elbows on the bar, swipes the drink a bartender sets in front of him—he must come here often—and talks around the straw. "So are you, like, really invested in solving that?"

"Oh." Stevie quits spinning her Rubik's cube to pass it from hand to hand. "Uh, no. I've almost solved it a couple times by accident, but. It helps with, um"—well, there's nothing else for it—"the anxiety? Just, like. Something else to focus on, I guess."

"Oh. Oh, yeah, sure, I—sorry. Shit." He laughs, a little flat, self-deprecating, and rotates his plastic cup around a napkin. "I'm, uh. Really smooth, can you tell?"

Is he... *trying* to be smooth? She's too into that notion for her own good, so Stevie plays it cool with a half-smile and a one-shouldered shrug, unsure of how much to commit to here. "It's a fair question."

Another laugh. "I appreciate the diplomacy. But, ah. I think I owe you a 'not actually fair, but you're too polite to say so' question now."

"That's pretty clever. Did you practice that in the mirror?"

"Is that your question?"

She shrugs again, both shoulders this time. "No take-backs."

"Well, in that case." Milo straightens, slaps his hands on the bar and starts drumming. "No. I just talk a lot, so I'm bound to say something *clever*, as you, again, so politely put it, every once in a while."

"Maybe I'm just relieved it wasn't about a yeast infection this time?"

And *another* laugh, this one full-bodied and real and it makes Stevie equal parts embarrassed and proud of herself.

"I *bet*. But I mean—is it like, creepy?" he wants to know. "That I'm so worried about that? I always have to tell people, y'know, I'm not a medical professional, but you should hear some of the stuff they'll jam up in there when they're left, uh. *Unsupervised*."

Morbidly intriguing. Stevie opens her mouth to say so, but the front door opens first.

"You've got to be kidding me," she mutters, barely audible over the raucous chatter of the sudden influx of wannabe frat boys. *Wannabe*, because while this is a college town, the college is small, mostly artsy, and notably lacking in any Greek system. Not that it stops these guys from *believing*, though.

That would be problem enough, but of course it's not *the* problem—no, *the* problem is that there's a few alumni with them. And, like she and Dottie manifested his presence, Erik Callahan is one of them.

"Ah." Milo glances over his shoulder. "Looks like the children are up past their bedtime."

Stevie would laugh, or point out that she's only got a couple of years on this crowd, or *something*, but it really is a *crowd*. Loud and sweaty and unfamiliar and her cue to leave. It's earlier than she'd planned or wanted, but that's the gamble you take when you exist while agoraphobic.

C'est la vie, or whatever.

"I should get going." Stevie takes a bill from her wallet and tucks it under the inside of the counter; she'll text Tatum, just in case, to make sure she gets it.

"Oh—really?" Milo blinks, surprised. "Are one of those guys, like, an ex-boyfriend, or—wait, shit, sorry—"

"No, it's okay," Stevie assures him. She slides off the stool, hitching her bag over her shoulder as she goes. "It's just—a lot of people?"

That's not the whole truth, but Stevie's not about to get into the *Erik* of it all. Anyway, Milo seems smart; maybe he'll put together the pieces of her extreme social anxiety without Stevie having to spill some big heart-to-heart about it. Or maybe he won't, and that's fine, too, she just wants to leave.

"Did you drive?"

Stevie shakes her head, wiggles her phone. "I'll get an Uber."

"You sure?"

"Um." She doesn't mean to, really, but she looks at the very quickly emptied drink in front of him. Milo clocks it.

"Oh. *Oh.* No, oh my God, I—this was just, uh. A Shirley Temple. And not a dirty one," Milo clarifies over tripping words and gesturing hands. "I, uh. I don't drink that much. Maybe a couple beers, sometimes, at home? Or sometimes more on special occasions. But. I didn't tonight, so."

He spreads his arms, goes for another grin. "Voilà, designated driver at your service."

As much as she needs to go, this guy keeps stopping her in her tracks. It's nothing uncomfortable, none of those things guys do when they can't take no for an answer. Milo seems about as flustered as Stevie is, awkward and trying not to be, which puts her more at ease if only for the solidarity of it all.

But *no one*'s ever as uncomfortable as Stevie is, so all she can do is stare at him and ask, confused, "But. Why?"

"I mean? This town and, uh, whereabouts?" Milo twirls a finger through the air. "We're not taking *technological advances* in stride. Uber'll cost you fifteen bucks for five minutes. *Plus tip.*

Far be it from me to tell you how to spend your money, this isn't personal, honestly this is mostly just about my strong opinions on the necessity of public transit."

He smiles, and it's—someone kill her, please—*endearing*, and Stevie hates her life more and more with every second. Because she can't talk herself out of something, when someone else is so insistently talking her into it.

So she's a sucker for peer pressure! *Fine.* As if it's her fault. She grew up on candy cigarettes, okay, she refuses to take responsibility.

And *did she mention* that she might be nursing the delicate beginnings of a crush here? At this point Milo could drive one of those cars with the really loud engines he revs at every stoplight for no reason, and she'd still get in it.

"If you're sure?" Stevie tugs at the strap of her bag, tightening it because she can't stay still. "Let me just—oh, hey, Dottie, I was just heading out."

"I figured." Dottie spares the college boys a disinterested look. "Sorry I was gone so long. We're picking apart popular psychology over there, I have *no* aspirations whatsoever, but I saw you with Milo so I figured you were doing okay. He's really just a personified worm on a string."

"I... Huh." Milo knocks his fists together thoughtfully. "Legitimately do not know what to do with that, Dottie, thanks."

"Anytime." She turns to Stevie. "Honestly cannot believe Erik showed up. Madison must have invited him, after all. Should you tell her, or should I?"

Stevie's gaze flicks to where Erik's found his way over to Madison. They sure made quick work of *canoodling*, sheesh. "Nothing to tell. I'm not getting involved."

"Mm. Classy move. Probably for the best." Dottie's bright brown eyes flit between Milo and Stevie now, like she's trying to figure something out. "So what's happening here? Do you two know each other?"

"We've met." Stevie had planned on telling Dottie about this whole unprecedented possible crush, just after she figured it out for herself. She doesn't want to suss it out right now, what with Milo standing *right here* and all, so she keeps it going. Deflects, even. "What about you guys?"

"Me and Artemis are roommates," Milo explains. He'd been looking Erik's way, but the crease between his eyebrows softens when he looks back at Stevie. "The dude who was at the store yesterday, that's Dottie's cousin."

"Oh, jeez. Small world."

"Honey, it's the *smallest*," Dottie agrees. A Cheshire cat grin dances across her berry mouth. Okay, so, Stevie doesn't know what all that's about, but Milo's shifting on his feet like it makes him nervous.

Huh.

"*Well*, kids, don't let me keep you," Dottie says, not giving them an inch but, then, Stevie didn't expect her to. "You good to give peach here a ride home, Milo?"

"Yeah." Milo nods. He scratches at a spot under his headband and makes it go crooked. "Yeah, absolutely, I was just luring her to my vehicle with, y'know, promises of candy."

"Hot fudge sundae Pop-Tarts," Stevie corrects him.

Milo nods some more. "Hot fudge sundae Pop-Tarts."

"Hm. You're both weird." Dottie wags a finger between them. "I dig that. Text me when you're home safe."

That could be construed as a *wink wink, nudge nudge*, but the truth is none of Stevie's friends are that subtle. All considered, she's grateful for that; she's all fluttery nervous as it is, the last thing she needs is some coy remark that's going to keep her up all night out of sheer mortification. But Dottie just wants a wellness text from them both, no innuendo about it.

Better get out of here before Tatum sees Stevie leaving with someone, though, lest she bust out more of the sexually explicit Running Man. Erik's too—ahem—*busy* to notice her, at least, thank God for small miracles and all that.

"Alrighty-o." Milo claps his hands, then sweeps an arm at the door. He gives Stevie that smile again, all crinkles around his eyes, and no she does *not* get all Jell-O around the knees, no, she's perfectly *fine*—

"Let's blow this popsicle stand, shall we?"

HOW MANY DEGREES OF SEPARATION ARE THERE BETWEEN KEVIN BACON AND YOUR LOVE LIFE?

T hank whichever divine entity might be listening, Milo's just glad he had the urge (and the *follow-through*) to clean his car this morning.

The Fiat Panda, circa 1986, looks good from the outside and runs like a dream—Milo works on it himself, it's a reliable car so he doesn't have to sweat it too much—but the inside tends to look like he lives there. Spare clothes, fast food wrappers and empty soda bottles, a few paperbacks he likes to keep handy in case the store's slow, the usual, but possibly off-putting to someone he doesn't know but very much *wants to*.

He's arguing with himself over whether or not he should open the door for that *someone*, but then Stevie does it herself. Ah, well. He cranks the driver's side window about halfway down, and Stevie follows suit on the passenger side.

He's learning some things about this girl and deducing a few others. His deductions include and are mostly limited to: one, Rubik's cube accounted for, she has some major social anxiety; two, judging by the *looks*, Dottie definitely knows Stevie's the girl he has a crush on, *thank you*, Artemis and the perils of the group chat; and three, she's got history with Erik.

Milo is admittedly—and as much as it *pains him* to admit—not thrilled about that last one. He wouldn't begrudge anybody their lousy romantic past, God knows he's got his own, but did it have to be *Erik*? Milo knows way too much about the dude's *sexual proclivities.* And he wouldn't begrudge anybody that, either, different strokes and all, but it's vastly uncool for him to have any insight into Stevie's sex life when she's none the wiser, right?

Also, Erik fuckin' sucks.

Be that as it may, what Milo's learned, without a doubt, is that Stevie knows Dottie and lives with Tatum, so she says when she gives him her address to plug into the GPS. And through all these not-even-six degrees of separation, somehow they've never met before. If he factors in Stevie's anxiety, that's probably why. She might not go out that much and, when she does, she goes home early, meanwhile Milo doesn't usually get out 'til late, such is the nature of his work schedule.

They've been *ships passing in the night* for who knows how long. Maybe there's something cosmically poetic about that, maybe it's just a dumb meaningless coincidence, maybe it's not even *that*—maybe it's just A Thing That Happened. Milo can't decide, and frankly the last thing he has time for in the midst of his sexual identity crisis is a faith-based one, too.

And in yet another feat of possible cosmic poetry, Stevie's the one to snap him out of it: "So, um. Does your car have a name?"

"Yeah, actually. I always think it's kind of a bummer when people don't name their stuff. Where's the *whimsy*, y'know? Anyway—"

Milo pulls onto the main road, headlights fighting the last of the sunset for attention. He can't spare Stevie too many glances while he drives; the strabismus wasn't a dealbreaker for his license, but the inhibited peripheral vision makes him less of a casual driver, more of a constantly alert and possibly a little paranoid one.

He knocks his thumb against the steering wheel. "This is Audrey II. Mostly because she's green. I thought about calling her Audrey III since that felt, I dunno." Milo rocks his hand from side-to-side against the wheel. "Somehow less derivative? Or something. But it doesn't sound as good."

"Too many Rs, maybe?" Stevie suggests.

"I think that must be it, yeah." He fishes the aux cord from its cupholder, offers it to her. "So we've got a... twenty-five-minute drive—yeesh, can't believe you were gonna pay an Uber, but, uh. Dealer's choice for music."

"Wouldn't you be the dealer?"

"Yeah, you know what, I guess that analogy doesn't hold up, but"—Milo shakes the cord at her—"I'll let it slide."

She hesitates. It's not just because the cord's still in his hand that he knows, but it's like Milo can *feel* her not being sure if she should take him up on it. He wonders if it's an anxiety thing; he's got it, too, but general, not social, so he's not sure where the overlap begins and ends.

He doesn't have to ask—and not that he would have—before Stevie takes the aux and plugs it into her phone. It's quick, like she did it by sheer force of will instead of thinking about it.

"I have some, um. *Eclectic* tastes." Her words are accompanied by that bubbly *schick-schick-schick* sound it makes when you scroll through music. "I can spare you, if you want, maybe put on this Top 40 playlist instead?"

"Absolutely not. What's eclectic? I mean, I know what it means," Milo clarifies as he turns down one of the backroads, "but give me an example."

"Oh, well. Uh. One time one of my playlists shuffled from 'Do Wah Diddy Diddy' to 'Ms. New Booty'? I think that's the most informative thing I could tell you."

Milo tries to whistle, but it pretty quickly tapers off into a laugh. "*What playlist* is that?"

"Bangers."

"*Bangers.*"

"Yeah. Y'know." She shrugs, taps her screen. "Songs that bang."

"Color me intrigued."

Stevie hums. "I thought so," she says, and then Hall & Oates hit the speakers. "'You Make My Dreams Come True' is actually why I made this playlist in the first place."

"Could've been the only song on *bangers* and still earned it."

"Right. But the playlist is actually…" Stevie taps her phone to wake up the screen, the bulb of bright light popping in the car's darkening interior. "Eleven hours long? Ish."

"So I need to take the scenic route to your place, is what you're saying."

"We could get to the world's biggest ball of yarn and back in about that time."

"You know where the world's biggest ball of yarn is?" Milo asks, impressed at that kind of offhand and odd (affectionate) factoid. "Like, down to the minute, you know where it is?"

"Well, there's more than one biggest ball of yarn. *Alleged* biggest ball of yarn. Or twine," Stevie corrects herself. She curls one leg underneath her, knee bumping the center console. "The one I'm talking about is in Kansas."

"Avid traveler?"

"Uh. No." The backroads are wide and empty, so Milo flicks a quick glance to his right to see Stevie shake her head. She leans an elbow on the door, chin in her hand. "No, I'm... kind of a homebody. But roadside attractions would be the thing to get me to go."

"Oh, I'd so do, like, a cross-country tour for some giant ketchup bottles."

"Do you travel a lot?"

"Eh." Milo rocks his hand again. "We did Disney maybe twice when I was a kid, but now it's just like, amusement parks are a hotbed of contagions and, also? Expensive as fuck. Where else is there to go? I don't hike, which is like *the thing to do* now, so any aspirations I might've had about Instagrammable vacations were, y'know, dead outta the gate. What else do people travel for?"

"I think we've established I'm not the person to ask."

"And I thought we were supposed to be a *team* here!" Milo says, with exaggerated affront.

Stevie laughs, more uninhibited than she did yesterday at the store. Satisfaction settles in the pit of Milo's gut and in the corners of his smile. The song shifts to one by the Four Tops.

"Alright, so our idea of a vacation is checking out enormous and *entirely ineffective* frying pans, and then maybe judging everyone else's Facebook posts about Universal Studios?"

"The lines are too long," Stevie says. She starts rambling a bit, like she's relieved to get this off her chest. "I don't even like when people are behind me in line at the grocery store, it makes me so nervous. I've left my phone or my wallet or something at the register so many times, just because I was trying to get out of the way so fast."

"The mortifying ordeal of being known?" Milo guesses.

"I know that's a real thing, like, um. Psychologically? Sociologically? But it's also just a fancy way of saying you don't want people to look at you, I think, so. Yeah, that's it."

"Well, I need to keep my eyes on the road"—Milo gestures at the windshield, at the long stretch of dusty backroad ahead of them—"so you're safe here. Unless something comes at us outta that cornfield, but you live in Indiana, so I assume you've got a contingency plan for that."

"Yeah. Whatever happens, happens."

Milo laughs at her deadpan tone. "You tellin' me you're not a *final girl*, Stevie Hart?"

"Not in this economy. Which crisis are we on, again? I'd rather be dead."

"I'm pretty sure we've all been in a perpetual state of crisis just, in general?" Milo knows the feeling all too well right now. "So, yeah, I think I'd probably go with nihilistic acceptance if the corn cryptids got me, too."

"Glad you see things my way," Stevie says, on another, quieter sort of chuckle that gets snatched up by the breeze and superseded by Ritchie Valens. (Incidentally, if Milo had to score his feelings for Stevie, the rhythm of his heart is definitely following the chaotic beat of "La Bamba.")

"So, uh." She stalls. It's something she seems to do a lot, like it's ingrained in her speech pattern. "I really appreciate the ride, but I'm sorry if I cut your night short. You were only there for, what, just a few minutes?"

Milo shrugs it off. "Give or take. I'm not worried about it, trust me. I've gotta work early, anyway, I really just swung by because I wanted to, uh." He coughs. "Ask Tatum something."

"About *lesbianism*," Stevie reiterates, dropping her voice in what Milo assumes is supposed to be an impression of him. It makes his lips twitch.

"*Right*. And you saw how that went."

"Maybe I can help." Her knee bumps the console again as she resituates. "I'm not a lesbian, I'm bi, but most people will tell you that means I'm 'half-gay.' It's *not* what it means, but..." She huffs, makes her mouth do that disgruntled horse noise. "Maybe I can help, anyway."

She could, since Milo was looking to get his *How do you know if you're attracted to girls?* conundrum answered. It's just... Well. This particular conundrum begins and ends with Stevie, so it feels disingenuous, somehow, to ask her.

And, truth be told, Milo doesn't feel like *discussing* his sexuality. The conversation takes a toll and he ends up discouraged whenever it doesn't click with people, and it usually doesn't click with people. He really does have to work early, too, so it's not like he's got all night to explain himself and then lose sleep over the fact that he didn't explain himself well enough.

But Stevie's waiting on an answer, waiting to *help*, and Milo can't come up with a good lie on the spot, so—"Alright, so how did you know you were into girls?"

"Oh, that's easy. I felt the same way about Ariel as I did Prince Eric, and when I was old enough to get the whole sexuality angle, I was just like, well"—she pops her lips—"guess I'm bi."

That is... pretty profoundly unhelpful. For Milo's purposes, anyway. But he *has to* ask, "You figured out your sexuality based on your *designs* towards cartoon characters?"

"Oh, shut up." She laughs. "I don't have a one-track mind, okay, I could write *dissertations* about that movie."

"Do tell."

"*First of all*," Stevie begins, thoroughly distracted as she straightens in her seat, ready to school him (which Milo is *very* much looking forward to, actually), "everyone thinks Ariel gave up her voice for a man, and the discussion pretty much begins and ends there, which is... No. She wanted to be human *before* Eric, so maybe her thing for him was opportunistic, even, but—whatever, I don't think that's it. He's a ten, he's got a good job, he literally risked his life for his dog, I don't see the problem."

"I'm on board."

"*Thank you.* So, *furthermore*—quit laughing, you asked me to do this—Eric's this representation of what Ariel wants, meanwhile he's in the same boat she is, isn't he? They're *parallels.*"

Stevie clasps her hands as if to demonstrate this fact. Milo hears her palms smack together. "Am I using that right? Kindred spirits, maybe, that's better. Because he's got responsibilities, he's got expectations riding on him, too, but all he wants is to *meet the right girl.* And, I mean, when you dig into both their motivations, isn't that what love is? It's being with someone who wants to give you what *you* want, like—it works because you *get* each other, you're there for each other.

"So, yeah, if you ask me, hating on that seems, you know"—now she's flapping her hands around, gesturing at nothing in particular—"really fucking backwards."

Milo would whistle, but his heart's a little bit lodged in his throat. "You weren't kidding about the dissertation."

"Absolutely I was not. I'm not even done, because, like, just to make sure I hit all the highlights here, it's not like Ariel's helpless, either. *Eric's* the damsel in distress. She's saving his himbo life, just, all over the place, and then they tag-team Ursula's straight-up murder."

"Couples who slay together stay together."

"I mean—" She laughs, this *what're-you-gonna-do?* sound. "*Yeah.* How many of these fairytale couples are actually killing the bad guy? But all anybody wants to talk about is how Ariel *gave up her voice.* I think that's missing the point. Or it's an oversimplification of the point."

"And the point is...?" Don't get him wrong, Milo knows where she's going with this, he'd just like to hear the closing argument.

Another huff, and Stevie slumps back into a more comfortable position. Her arms are crossed in defiance like she expects Milo to argue with her (he wouldn't dream of it). "They're both dumb, hot, equal opportunity murderers who believe in the power of *true love.* How that movie didn't make all of us bisexual is the real question."

Not an unfair conclusion, honestly. Milo's going to be mulling this one over for the foreseeable future (*reeling* over it, even, because Stevie's Thoughts and Feelings are hitting a little too relatable, somehow, and now he's got this creeping sensation that's usually associated with soul-searching).

For the *immediate* future... he's gonna need a minute.

"So, uh. Is there a '*second of all*' in there somewhere?"

"Just wherever it would naturally go, I got too excited."

Milo laughs. He checks all sides of the next intersection before he hangs left down another backroad. "You're a weird chick."

"A-*ha!*" She snaps her fingers. "But I'm not hearing I'm *wrong*."

"Well, I don't have a death wish," he teases, as deadpan as he can. She's better at that than he is. "Besides, I'm more of a Cinderella guy myself, but you're definitely right."

"Oh, *interesting*."

"Yeah, what can I say, I respect a girl who just wants a night off. Not her fault some dude's so obsessed with her he launches a full-scale manhunt so he can wife her up. Imagine the toll that took on the kingdom's resources." Milo whistles. "Like, talk about economic collapse, he was *all in*. I'd marry the guy, too."

"Is that why you were asking? About the attraction thing." Milo keeps his eyes forward, but he can feel Stevie looking at him. "Has a member of some royal family raised taxes in an effort to get your attention? Maybe? Because that might be an email scam."

He still can't come up with a lie, and it's not like he can take the excuse she offered since that's a *joke*, so Milo tries to laugh it off: "Ah, I dunno. Just curious, I guess. Though I *am* partial to a pyramid scheme, so I'd probably be into that."

"Milo. How many Nigerian princes are you sponsoring?"

"Oh, seventeen. At *least*."

"And you know those are all just guys from, like, Idaho or something, right?"

"I have a very giving heart."

Stevie laughs again, like it's all she ever does. It makes this funny little thrum go off in his chest, the kind of funny little thrum that hasn't been there in a long time. Long enough that he'd forgotten what it felt like, jaded enough that he'd forgotten that it can feel *good*.

Milo chances another look at Stevie. She's got her hand out the window, riding the breeze to the tune of another Four Tops song. A few flyaways dance around her temples, around her mouth, as she murmurs along to the lyrics on the radio.

And he just *knows* that he's in some kind of trouble here. He's going to have to rescind his shun on the group chat whether he likes it or not, he can't do this alone.

The trouble only gets worse when he pulls up to her curb. Now there's this funny twist—funnier than the thrum, even—in his gut, like all his nervous butterflies are coiled together and ready to spring—but not yet; first they want to make him sick and *then* they'll bust his chest wide open. You know, just to make matters worse, add insult to injury, life is hell, etc.

He cuts the engine, promptly making matters worse all on his own. There's nothing to distract him now, no rumble of the engine or Fine Young Cannibals—and who does Milo think he is, anyway, to cut off the Fine Young Cannibals in the middle of the chorus (or *ever*, for that matter)—but it seems like the right thing to do. If he sits there idling, Stevie will probably think he's eager for her to leave so he can get the hell out of here. Which, fine, is true in the sense that he doesn't want her to see him combust with nervous energy, but mostly he could sit here with her all night.

A racket of crickets filters through their open windows, and the obvious sounds of a backyard party nearby—indecipherable conversation, laughter, muffled music and the sharp sounds of snapdragons crackling against the pavement. Complete silence would be *exponentially* worse. So maybe the universe is at least marginally merciful, after all.

"Well, um." Stevie drops the aux cord back into its cupholder. "Thanks for the ride. And for indulging my rambling."

Milo looks at her. It's just light enough still for him to catch the twitch in her lips, a self-deprecating kind of smile. That twist in his gut tightens, and—

Oh. Wait. Okay. He gets what this is.

He wants to kiss her.

(More specifically, he wants to know what she had to drink tonight, and he wants to find out by tasting what's left of it on her tongue. He wants to know if she uses lip balm and what kind it is. Would she put her hands in his hair, on his chest, on his waist?

(Or maybe she'd just punch him in the face, you never know, because *Milo* wants to know all these things but the only way to know if Stevie does too would be to ask her, and he *can't do that*.)

He can't; he can't do that, that would be like... categorically insane. It doesn't matter what his insides are doing—that's a medical issue, probably—he can't just haul off and kiss this girl he's met all of twice, one of which was in a *professional capacity*.

Also? It's been a *hot* minute, okay, he's not entirely sure he knows what to do with his mouth anymore.

He certainly doesn't have any control over it, as it turns out, because the next thing he knows he's blurted out, clumsy and scrambling—

"Would you—can I see you again?" Oh, *God* damn it, could he be any more *overwrought* about it? Milo clears his throat. "I mean, like, do you maybe wanna hang out, swap some more feminist readings of childhood movies, maybe you can, uh, continue to expand my musical horizons... That, uh, that sort of thing?"

Stevie's lips don't just twitch this time, no, her mouth splits into the *biggest* smile. She's got a dimple in her right cheek. Jesus, Milo would buy real estate in that dimple.

"*Yeah*, I mean—yeah, here—" It's Stevie's turn to clear her throat as she fumbles for her phone, swipes the screen and hands it over. "Put your number in, I'll text you."

And Milo would stare at his phone until she did or until his eyes glazed over, whichever came first, but—*God bless*—Stevie texts him right away. It's the Groucho glasses emoji, because (shrug) "I never get to use that one."

"Just start tagging all your texts with it," he suggests, "like a signature."

"You think I should sign all my texts?"

"That's what my dad does. So I 'know it's him.'"

She hums thoughtfully. "I always wanted to be a dad."

"Well, see, there you go." Milo shoots her a text, the star-eyes emoji because "I never get to use that one."

"Come on, you can always use that one!" Stevie insists. "Don't tell me nothing and nobody's putting stars in your eyes, Milo, that's such a buzzkill."

"Is that so?" Milo can feel how much he's smiling, it almost hurts (how *do* you do it, Barbie?). "That's a hell of a line. You sure you have anxiety?"

"I—" Stevie whimpers, embarrassed, then chuckles, acquiescent. "Shut up. That was... not on purpose."

"Hey! It's fine!" Milo makes a show of waving his hands, dispelling her embarrassment whilst gloating about it (this is flirting, right?). "I have anxiety and I have to talk to *grown adults* about the difference between a clit and a G-spot—"

"Talk about *lines*—"

"*My point is*—oh my God." Milo chokes on his next laugh. Stevie smirks like she's won something. "That was *also* not on purpose, I just mean, like—God damn it." He drops his hands on the steering wheel. "We contain multitudes, or whatever. Anxiety does not stop us from being deviants."

Actually, Milo's not really predisposed to *deviancy*, but, whatever, he's trying to flirt with her. Stevie's already scrambled all his notions of what it means to be demisexual; he might as well use the confusion to his advantage before he inevitably panics about it.

"Probably something we should ask Dottie about," she says.

"Yeah," Milo agrees, "but we gotta buy her like, lunch or something. If she keeps spilling therapy for free, I think she gets to kick us in the shins."

"The unofficial Hippocratic oath."

Milo tilts his head at her, teasing. "I... don't think so?"

"Whatever." Stevie clicks her door open. "You're not a doctor."

"You are just"—what else can he say? So he says, dripping with moon-eyed affection—"so weird."

"Well, I don't get out much." Stevie's got one foot out the door, checking her bag to make sure she's got everything. "You'll see, now that I have your number."

"Is that a *threat*?"

"I'm going to text you every eighteen minutes, I have nothing better to do."

Milo taps his heart (the thing's going nuts). "I'm honored to be your nothing better to do."

"Now *that*"—Stevie hops out of the car, shuts the door, and points at him through the open window—"is a line."

Yeah. Milo grins, deeply pleased with himself, as he waits on the curb for Stevie to get inside safe. Maybe it was.

***

DOTTIE: It's STEVIE.

ARTEMIS: I'm sorry, were we in the middle of a conversation I don't know about?

DOTTIE: The girl Milo likes. They just left Loretta's together. You didn't recognize her at the store?

ARTEMIS: OH.
O h .
I thought she looked familiar, but I was so unceremoniously booted from the premises that I didn't have a chance to connect the dots.

DOTTIE: Talk about wasting my time!

ARTEMIS: Hey, I've never formally MET HER. I've caught a glimpse and then, poof, she disappears into the ether whenever there's too many people around
Which, like, *slay*
But I am not going to be responsible for your attitude

PENN: isn't that tatum's roomie? she's CUTE.

PENN: caaaaaan't believe i'm missing this.

ARTEMIS: That's what you get for leading your fabu life as a starving artist who has to spend all their free time networking, thus abandoning us little people

PENN: i /am/ in the middle of another aperol spritz, so ig i can't contest that.

ARTEMIS: And you're wearing a Thelma & Louise neck scarf, I saw your Insta. As usual, you disgust me, now back to the matter at hand......

ARTEMIS: They LEFT together?????????

DOTTIE: Don't be a freak, it's not like I caught them going at it in the bathroom.

PENN: please tell me he's not in this gc

DOTTIE: Cookie honey sweetie pie. Give me some credit, I'm a professional. He's been pointedly left out.

PENN: perfect. so are we taking bets re: the state of our dear friend's virginity after this fateful evening? that sounds like something we'd do.

ARTEMIS: If that girl pops his cherry I'm buying her a car.

DOTTIE: What did I just say about not being a freak?

ARTEMIS: DOROTHY. You didn't see his face when he got a look at her. I've never seen a man so desperate in my LIFE.

DOTTIE: Trust me, I just got an eyeful, I get it. He's full heart-eyes emoji.
But leave that boy and his virginity alone.

ARTEMIS: I KNOW it's a social construct, I am just

ARTEMIS: *typing...*

ARTEMIS: Okay fine so I'm a freak

DOTTIE: Mmmmhmmm.

***

MILO: alright so when you said "eclectic" ig i wasn't expecting smthn called ELECTRO SWING

STEVIE: !!!!!! it's one of my *favorites*

MILO: pretty sure this is what a panic attack sounds like
i should have stuck with bangers

STEVIE: well see i've got something for everyone, including my anxiety

MILO: that's fair. can't leave out the wee beasties that live in our brains

STEVIE: gotta keep 'em appeased like ancient gods, lest we incur their wrath

MILO: ur right ur right. i take back my initial disparaging comment

electro swing is in fact paramount to our brain chemistry

STEVIE: i knew you'd come around

MILO: ur powers of persuasion know no bounds, truly

STEVIE: ʺ^ ^ʺ

***

STEVIE: WHERE ARE YOU

TATUM: Depends on what you want

STEVIE: i just wanna talk

TATUM: Mmmm that's code for 'I'm going to kill u with my bare hands', so

TATUM: *Number Not Available*

STEVIE: i juuuuust wanna talk to you

TATUM: I can literally HEAR how menacing you mean that I didn't leave my clothes in the washer again, did I?

STEVIE: yes but dw i already spun them again and put them in the dryer. this isn't about mildew, it's about smthn else

TATUM: You might as well be speaking in riddles

STEVIE: these aren't riddles, i'm just being generally cryptic

TATUM: Is this a sex thing, is that why you can't be normal?

STEVIE: *typing...*

STEVIE: *typing...*

STEVIE: *typing...*

TATUM: I'll take that as a yes, we'll talk soon x

BANISHING DEMONS WITH THE ULTIMATE TEEN COMEDY SOUNDTRACK

I t's a full three days before Stevie sees Tatum again.

That's not totally unusual. Stevie's the homebody, but Tatum is in and out like the tides. She works two jobs—nights at Loretta's, days at the gym—and she likes to be *out*.

To each their own. It's just that *right now* Stevie has a bone to pick with her best friend and she's nowhere to be found.

And, sure, Stevie could double-triple-quadruple text Tatum her laundry list of questions about Milo—first and foremost *how dare you never tell me you were acquainted with the love of my life, I'm pretty sure*. Not really a question, but Stevie has to marvel at the sheer *nerve*.

Is she being dramatic? *Maybe*. But she also hasn't left the house in three days, so these things happen.

Besides, it's a conversation made for margaritas straight from their cheap plastic blenders. That's the thing about having a crush, is that half the fun's in the atmosphere of telling people about it.

(Maybe even *all* of the fun, in the all-too-often event that the crush goes on unrequited and you're left to wonder what was even the point. *The point is* overly-tequila'd homemade margaritas with your friends. Stevie's not going to give that up just for the potential of quicker answers.)

When she wakes up on Sunday morning to the sound of the shower, Stevie doesn't bother to make herself presentable. Her hair's still in its overnight topknot, she's filmed in dry sweat underneath her sleep cardigan and Oscar the Grouch shorts, feet stuffed hastily in her Homer Simpson head slippers. She studies them with a morbid sort of curiosity as she paces the hallway outside the bathroom, marveling at the aesthetic of a cartoon character swallowing her feet whole, while she prepares to accost her roommate as soon as she opens that door.

Of course, she did make Tatum a smoothie first. While she may have her fair share of problems with her mom, the woman didn't raise Stevie to be an animal. Trading Tatum a smoothie for the chance to berate her is The Right Thing To Do.

So, naturally, Tatum isn't the one who opens the bathroom door.

"Oh, son of a bitch," Stevie curses, and starts drinking the smoothie herself. She should have jumped the gun and loaded up the cheap plastic blender with margarita instead.

Whitney's wearing last night's outfit and a smile. What Stevie assumes is last night's outfit, anyway, a cute sequined top and pleather leggings; and it's less of a smile, more of a simper, but with Whitney it's the best you're going to get.

"Hiiiiii, Nicky." Whitney's the only one who calls her that, a play on Stevie Nicks that she used to find charming and flattering, because it couldn't be anything but, right?

But that was *once*, before Stevie knew better. The truth is Whitney Preston—of the Peach Avenue Prestons, which means absolutely nothing and yet there's a certain small-town clout to it—is mostly just kind of mean, in that passive-aggressive, condescending way that's really easy to make fun of, but only *after* your feelings aren't so freshly fucking eviscerated.

(And, no, the nickname doesn't hurt Stevie's feelings, but she *is* suspicious about it these days.)

"Why are you here," Stevie says flatly, not even a question because she knows exactly why Whitney's here. It's not like it's hard.

Because she's unbearably hot, with her curves and her thick blonde ringlets, coiled like the perfect curly fry (damp now from the shower, but you can just *tell* how effortlessly springy they are) and her Disney princess brown eyes—and so, clearly, her on-again, off-again thing with Tatum is *on* again.

Although, "Why are you here, on this planet" would also be a fair question, in Stevie's opinion.

"*Nicky*." Whitney clucks, pouts, and taps her on the nose. Stevie swats her hand away. "Come on, sweetie, I know you missed me. What's it been, two months?"

"Four and a half." Stevie turns tail towards the kitchen, flings her arms out, possibly splattering the wall with smoothie debris from the open top of the blender. "But who's counting!"

"You're such a *grump*."

Bah. She doesn't need to listen to this.

Stevie connects her phone to the Bluetooth speaker in the kitchen, promptly raising Whitney's *grump* with a far-too-loud onslaught of the Mighty Mighty Bosstones from her *girl, turn off the snooze and eat some breakfast* playlist.

Whitney grimaces at the volume. "I hate when you do this!"

Stevie flips her off with both hands while she shimmies sort-of to the beat and backwards—her trusty Homer Simpson slippers have good traction for shimmying that doesn't result in bodily harm—around the kitchen.

"You're so *annoying*," Whitney gripes. Stevie keeps dancing and pretends not to hear her. "*Nicky!*"

"Huh?" She keeps moving her feet, but pauses in the middle of her completely unrhythmic voguing to cup a hand around her ear. "Sorry, what'd you say? You're leaving?"

Whitney's so close to stomping her foot, Stevie can practically taste it. "You *know* that's not what I said!"

Stevie makes a show of furrowing her brow. It's not *totally* put-upon, even a mediocre moonwalk takes *focus*, but she can hear Whitney perfectly fine. Too fine, even. Stevie would rather never hear her again.

"You're such a bad hostess."

"Uh"—Stevie shimmies past her, arms aloft like one of those wacky waving inflatable arm-flailing tube men, way off the beat now—"whatever, I didn't invite you here."

"You could still be *hospitable.*"

"*Nope.*" She skids to a stop in front of the fridge. It's too early for margaritas, fine; she's sure they've got the makings for screwdrivers around here (which surely can't be better or worse than tequila before noon, duh, but it's all about the *presentation.* You put hard liquor in some orange juice, *holy loophole, Batman!*, it's all part of a balanced breakfast).

Bingo, they're stocked on knock-off Tropicana and vodka. Stevie pops the tops on both.

While she's prepping her blood/alcohol level for a morning full of Whitney, the problem in question grabs her phone from the counter and adjusts the volume to something reasonable. At least she didn't turn it off.

But for every act of mercy there's an act of... hubris, maybe? Because for a blissful half-second there, Stevie didn't imagine anything would go wrong. She was even starting to relax after the shock of finding Whitney in her bathroom, only for the universe to say "Um, no, actually, remember you haven't been relaxed since the womb, and probably not even then. You're not starting now."

All that to say, Stevie's phone chirps with an incoming text, and Whitney reads it.

(And, by the way? Dick move.)

Her eyebrows go up and Stevie snatches the phone. It's from Milo, but she clicks out of it before she can read the message. She's not about to try flirting when Whitney's hanging around.

"Speaking of which..." Whitney pops a hip against the counter. "Heard you left Loretta's with Milo the other night. Didn't know y'all were *talking*."

Stevie considers the vodka in her hand. Maybe she should just waterfall it.

"Yeah," she says, pouring a generous helping into her rainbow tin mug. "He gave me a ride home, that's all."

She's not sure why she feels the need to explain herself. Whitney's not asking because she actually cares; she only cares about the relationship statuses of people she wants to sleep with, which is fair enough. She and Stevie have never been each other's type, and Stevie would guess that Milo doesn't qualify, either. Whitney's taste in guys veers more along the lines of Madison's—that is to say, their standards are less of a high bar and more like a limbo stick that never gets off the ground.

Even if Whitney did care, it's none of her business, so. No explanation needed. Nope.

Stevie splashes orange juice—disproportionately not quite as much as the vodka—into her mug and takes a healthy draw. *Gooooood* morning.

"Hm. Hm hm hm." Whitney mixes her own screwdriver in a thick-cut hot pink glass Stevie found at Goodwill for fifty cents. "So is he your new guy?"

Oh, she is not answering that even a little bit.

"I'd get it, if he were," Whitney goes on. She leans back against the counter, sipping daintily from her glass. "I'm just saying, you know, been there."

Her eyes roll and so does Stevie's stomach. "You've got your work cut out for you, that's all I'm gonna say."

"Why say anything at all?" Stevie asks dully. She doesn't expect an answer, mostly because Whitney never takes her seriously.

And, right, she just *titters*. "Oh, never mind. I'm probably blowing it out of proportion, but—well. You'll see what I mean soon enough, I'm sure."

Okay, so this cryptic shit is super unsettling. Stevie sees what Tatum was talking about now, and she resolves to never do it again. In fact... fuck it, she's not doing whatever *this* is, either.

"Well, Whit, it's been real." Stevie gathers her mug and phone, and as she makes her abrupt (and still shimmying) exit from the kitchen, she kicks up the volume on a Barenaked Ladies song—Whitney *hates* the Barenaked Ladies, because she has no taste—and locks herself in her room.

Stevie rolls onto her bed, settling into unmade blankets to enjoy her petty, *petty* victory (sponsored by Bluetooth speakers). She opens her messages, laugh-reacts to another "dun-dun" meme Milo sent. Their mutual obsession with SVU always gives them something to talk about, bless you, Mariska.

She aimlessly scrolls her socials and purposefully skips to more songs she knows Whitney doesn't like. All the while she bobs her feet to the music, only slightly muffled by her closed door, and nurses her oversized mug of screwdriver, waiting for Tatum to wake up and play mediator.

Or, more likely, walk Whitney out to her car and then come back to give Stevie what-for. Which is, like, *unfair*, since their roles were supposed to be reversed this morning, until Tatum went and ruined it with another hook-up with literally the worst kind of person to hook up with.

She's not going to think about the possibility that Milo might have done likewise, however once-upon-a-time it might've been.

Just as she's totally definitely not thinking about it, her lock clicks open and there Tatum is, wriggling the skeleton key between her fingers. She uses it to point over her shoulder, back to where the music's coming from. "Whitney says you're responsible for the, uh, *ruckus*?"

"She doesn't like *Bruce Springsteen*." Stevie scoffs so hard she almost chokes on it. "What is she, a Republican?"

"*Language.*" Tatum wrinkles her nose, then smirks it away as she leans on the doorjamb. "We're gonna go to brunch. You wanna come?"

Stevie musters up the *drollest* face she can. Tatum lifts her hands in surrender. "Okay, then I've got about two minutes for you before I bounce. What's your problem?"

What's your problem, what's wrong with you... Stevie's starting to think she's got some major soul-searching to do, if her friends keep talking to her like this.

But! That can wait! Stevie chucks one of her pillows and hits Tatum straight in the face.

"Ten points!" she declares with victorious hands in the air. Then she picks up her mug, points it at Tatum. "I don't have a problem. You are the problem. You can't just let Whitney *into our house.* She'll keep trying to come back!"

"Okay, I'm going to need more than two minutes to defend my sex life to you." Tatum tosses the pillow back on the bed. "Tell me what the deal is with yours. Is this the bacon club Chalupa problem? Does it have something to do with Milo giving you a ride on Wednesday?"

She dances on the tips of her toes. "*What kind of ride was it, Stevie?*"

Hilarious. Stevie only just manages not to wallop her with the pillow again. "Yes, he's the bacon club Chalupa problem. I met him at Nobody's and just, lost control of my life. Why didn't you *tell me* about him?"

"Milo? I mean—huh." Tatum thinks it over. "Well, he doesn't really date, I don't think? I've never seen him with anybody, and he definitely never leaves with anyone."

"Are you sure? Maybe he has and you just didn't notice."

"No, you know we have to keep track of who's doin' who and who's pissed off about it."

"You *have to*?"

"For entertainment value."

"That is *sick*."

"That's capitalism," Tatum corrects her. "I get paid four dollars an hour, I can get my sick kicks however I want."

She gets paid eighteen dollars an hour, but those are still some poverty wages, believe it or not, so Stevie lets it go. She taps her fingers nervously around her mug. "Whitney never said anything?"

"About Milo? No." Tatum shakes her head. "Why? She said she mentioned him to you, but what did she say? Specifically."

Great, now Tatum seems just as nervous. She's not the easily ruffled kind, but Whitney's always brought out the insecure part of her; it's why they break up so often.

"Nothing really *specific*," Stevie clarifies, not really clarifying at all since Whitney didn't give her much to go on. "Just some insinuation that she's been there, done that. You know how she is, she'll say something *mysterious* and then it's all 'Oh, never mind, L-O-L, see you in hell.'"

Tatum sighs. "Can you at least pretend to be cool with her?"

Stevie blows a raspberry. "Can she at least pretend to not be an asshole?"

"Maybe she went out with him?" Tatum suggests, *unhelpfully*. "*I've* never seen him with anyone, but I've only been at Loretta's for, what, two years? And that's where I met her, so. Could've been before then."

Hm. Must've been. Stevie scratches the side of her nose. None of this should bother her—she *just met* Milo, it stands to reason that he's dated before her, and it's not like they're even *dating*. He sold her a sex toy and gave her a ride home from the bar; it's not exactly a joint taxes kind of situation, more like swapping memes. It's just...

God. Why did it have to be *Whitney*? She can *oh, never mind* it all she wants, but Stevie doesn't buy that for a second. It's like Dottie said—that's all just Whitney's way of seeming *aloof* and *interesting* and also she's *fucking insane* and really, honestly, Erik would be perfect for her because they're both the worst people Stevie knows. They'd be volatile and dramatic and they'd break up every other week, but it would save everyone else the trouble of dating them, so, win-win.

But, no. Whitney just had to come home with Tatum again, and now suddenly this is Stevie's problem.

"So are you guys dating again, or...?"

"I don't know." Tatum shrugs. Her momentary insecurity has passed and she's back to (trying to be) blasé about it. "Honestly I just really wanted to make out with someone, and she's a good kisser."

"Yeah. Well. I guess you know she's not gonna harvest your liver and disappear into the night," Stevie has to admit, however begrudgingly.

"Babe, turn off the SVU, maybe try a nice romcom every once in a while. But yes." Tatum blows her a kiss. "See ya."

That conversation wasn't super helpful. But—the front door opens and shuts, leaving behind the heavy, relieving silence of being alone (aside from the Blessid Union of Souls coming from the kitchen)—at least Whitney's not in the house anymore.

The door opens again about five seconds later, but before Stevie has a chance to worry about it, Dottie's waltzing into her bedroom. She's wearing sweats and a cropped *Daria* tee, bringing along the scent of her eucalyptus lotion, and toast and bacon, courtesy of the paper bag in her hand.

She tosses Stevie a foil-wrapped breakfast sandwich. "Don't tell me Tatum's back at it with Regina George."

"Fine, I won't tell you."

"Son of a *bitch*."

"I'll give you my rock collection if you date her instead." Stevie takes a generous bite of her sandwich, scattering crumbs all down her front. "Either of them, actually, I'm not picky."

Dottie snorts, hops into Stevie's bed, and unwraps her own sandwich. "First of all, I don't want your rock collection, what is wrong with you? Rocks belong outside."

Hey. It's a nice rock collection. Stevie paints bugs on them. They kinda look like a toddler painted them, but they're *cute*.

"You use *crystals*."

"*Second of all*," Dottie says, more forcefully as she pretends that Stevie didn't say anything, "don't forget that I am blessedly asexual and happily married. I don't want anything to do with this."

True. It's not like Stevie could forget Dottie's partner in crime and other milestones. Rusty Beckett is big and loud and he plays a killer banjo in a bar-hopping bluegrass band. They're not *exactly* an odd couple, but you wouldn't put two and two together until you actually saw them together; *then* it's obvious, just not before. They could make anyone believe that love is the real deal.

"Neither do I, but..." Stevie swishes her drink around. "Whitney said something about Milo."

"Of course she did." Dottie plucks the mug from Stevie's grip and takes a swig. "Shit, no wonder you needed that. What is this, straight vodka?"

"There's a suggestion of orange juice."

Dottie smacks her lips. "More like a distant memory of orange juice, maybe. But, look, don't worry about whatever she said. Whitney's a dumbass. She's just trying to psych you out."

Well, sure. But—ugh. *Ugh*, aurgh, etc. Stevie doesn't want to be *that person*, but Whitney's prettier than her, she's charming and sociable and she knows how to bat her eyelashes in a way that is somehow not ridiculous. Yeah, she sucks most of the time, but even so she's the kind of person that other people want to fuck.

And maybe it's bullshit, but being the kind of person that other people want to fuck makes you worth something. Stevie could pick apart everything that's wrong with that all she wants, but it doesn't change the fact of the matter.

"Stop thinking so loud." Dottie polishes off the rest of her sandwich. "You know you can ask me about him, right? Milo. He's a friend, not a patient, I can tell you whatever I want. I actually feel like a fuckin' clown that I didn't try to set y'all up before, but... Mm."

She brushes crumbs off her fingertips. "The thing about Whitney is, she's the last person he dated. Or, *talked to*, I don't think things progressed much from the talking stage. That went on for a few weeks and then I don't know what happened, he wouldn't talk about it, but it flatlined. He's been out of the dating scene since."

Stevie's not sure if this is making her feel better or worse. She gnaws on a piece of bacon, more anxious than hungry. "Do you think maybe he's still into her?"

"Oh—" Dottie laughs, but like it's not all that funny. "That's a *hard* no. It's been three years, and whatever happened, it messed him up. I think Whitney probably talked some mad shit to him about—well, I'll tell you this because it's not exactly a secret, but Milo's demisexual. And he's into you. *And* he's confused about it. That's why he's so spastic. Which I say with love," Dottie's quick to add, "but being demi can get complicated, so they're all a little unhinged."

Oh.

Stevie has a vague understanding of what demisexual means—someone whose sense of sexual attraction isn't based on the physical, right? She could see how that gets confusing, complicated, all that, especially for a guy, since men are born and bred to be hypersexual to the nth and absolutely bonkers degree. They're "supposed to" have sex on the brain like it's an involuntary urge.

Most people have similar assumptions about bisexuals, so, Stevie can relate to the bullshit. She definitely does not want to fuck everyone she meets; she doesn't even want to fuck a modest percentage of the people she meets. In part because so many of them think she does, which would be laughable if it weren't so *annoying.*

That must be why Milo asked about attraction—because he's attracted to *her.* If what Dottie's saying is true, and Dottie's no liar.

Stevie has to bury her face in her pillow and scream to get all of her pent-up feelings out. It's mostly excitement and nerves and a dash of thinking about how Whitney totally sucks.

"There you go," Dottie encourages her. "See, don't you feel better when you let me tell you things?"

Stevie drops the pillow into her lap, gives it a few satisfying whacks. "I was just trying to, I don't know, sort myself out before

I asked? You know dating's just, not been working for me lately. I don't remember the last time I actually *liked* someone."

"Well, you picked a good one, if it's any consolation. We love a demisexual," Dottie says. "None of that playboy shit. I mean, please, I don't trust a man who's wildly sexually experienced. Who has the time? Get a job."

Unequivocally true. Stevie's been with a couple of people with vast experience, and they've definitely been her worst times. They go in way too self-assured, always thinking they know what she wants, what's going to *do the trick*, without asking.

Sometimes it's fine, she guesses, but mostly it's awkward at best, because they're doing their thing and you're just lying there like, "Huh. This is weird." And they think your scrunchy face is what you look like when you're about to come, but really you're trying to figure out how to politely tell them to stop *strumming your vagina* to what you suspect is the tune of "Wonderwall," please, without hurting their feelings.

(...Or is that not a universal experience? *Anyway.*)

"So, um." Stevie pops the last bite of sandwich into her mouth, less anxious now. Not completely *un*-anxious, but she's not convinced that's possible, anyway. "Any advice?"

"Oh, he's *besotted*," Dottie assures her, and Stevie's anxiety flares again but this time it's in a good way. "I think you're set. I will tell you, though, it's like this—"

Dottie wriggles comfortably into the pillows. "You know how people say, like, 'You just need to meet the right person' and it sounds like puritanical bullshit? Well, that's how it actually is for demis most of the time. Anybody on the asexual spectrum, we're stuck in this liminal space. We're not celibate—celibacy's a choice, not an orientation—but we're not what sex-positive people want us to be, either.

"Not to throw my PhD around or anything"—Dottie clears her throat importantly, and rightly so—"but I'm gonna. Being sex positive doesn't mean you *just* support sex. I think a lot of times it comes off as very 'yas, queen, slut it up!', but that's not the all-encompassing thing of it. It means you support *everyone's* orientation, and you celebrate how they live with it.

"The point is to eradicate shame, because no one should feel ashamed of wanting sex, or not wanting it, or however else they feel about it. But really what's happening is that we went from one extreme to another. So now if you're not into sex, or if you're sex-repulsed, you're repressed, a prude, under the influence of religious trauma, blah-fucking-blah."

Dottie sighs, waves it off. "I can't tell you the gross goddamn *nonsense* I get for being trans and asexual. Some of these people really try to tell me 'Honey, you don't have to abstain! You're totally hot, you're such a powerful woman, you should embrace that.' Of course I'm hot. That has nothing to do with anything. They think they've got good intentions, but really it's just... *ew*, you know?"

"Patronizing?" Stevie suggests, because fucking *ew*, indeed.

"And hella aphobic," Dottie tacks on. "I'm not asexual because I'm harboring some deep self-esteem issues about being trans. That's not how being asexual works. At *all*. I just happen to be both. And it's really nobody's business, but you know how people are when, y'know, again, they think they've got good intentions."

Stevie nods. Her experiences with those people are to a lesser degree than what Dottie deals with, but she gets it.

"Now, I'm telling you all this just to *really* tell you, that we on the ace spectrum can't win," Dottie continues. "We'll get there, but right now? We exist in this dimension of things heteronormative people and most queer people don't get. Like, this is the only time these groups seem to agree on anything. Honest, I can't even come up with a joke thing.

"So as far as things with you and Milo go, what I'm getting at, really, is just…" Dottie twitches her fingers in the air, searching for the right way to put it. "Be careful with him, okay? Dating doesn't make a lot of sense to him. He pretends he's got it all under control, but he's breakable like a Precious Moments doll. He's got the big doleful eyes and everything."

A chuckle shakes its way past Stevie's lips. "Yeah, I will." She picks at a loose thread in her purple plaid comforter. "Be careful, I mean. I think I, um. I think I like him a lot. I don't want to mess that up."

"You won't, peach." Dottie burrows a hand in Stevie's hair, tips her forward so she can plant a kiss there, too. "Take it from the blissfully happy married lady, okay? I think you two could have something really good going on."

Stevie thinks about the way she feels around Milo—and, yes, okay, it's only been a couple of times, but she feels *light* and *easy* and she doesn't worry about looking stupid. Nerves flutter around her stomach and sometimes her face feels hot, but it's not in that sick nauseous way that makes her burrito-blanket herself until she's squeezed all of the bad feelings out. No, with Milo her nerves are… *giggly*?

Yeah. *Giggly* feels about right.

And if that's not something really good going on, Stevie doesn't know what is.

SELF-ACTUALIZATION IS UNATTAINABLE (AND YET...!)

T hings have gotten pretty bizarre, very fast.

Milo doesn't mean to *oversell* it or anything, but give him a break, okay? This is the first time in three years he's been even cautiously interested in the vague possibility of someone—ah, *romance*! But. *Three years.* He has friends who routinely experience debilitating ennui whenever they haven't gotten laid in a month.

(Which, by the way? Fucking ridiculous. Maybe it's the demi-sexuality of it all. Hell, call him a virgin who can't drive, even—it's half-right, at least, and has there ever been a more cutting insult than Brittany Murphy's delivery of this line?—but Milo really cannot comprehend how sex can be *that* life-changing. Something with the brain chemicals, probably, but if that's the case... Damn. Just. Take your meds.)

It's been a week and a half since he met Stevie. A whopping twelve days, and already he's in way over his head. Pretty sure he never *wasn't* in over his head here.

But now it's *worse*. Because now he has her number, and all of a sudden it's like he can't get through the day without talking to her. It's *bananas*—too fast, too soon, codependent *bananas*.

He hasn't seen Stevie since he gave her a ride home—he's been picking up shifts between the store and the auto shop, mayhaps a little desperate to bank some vacation time—and he's, like, obsessed with her. This is either the great love of his life, or the misleading beginning of a made-for-TV thriller, *who's to say*.

He can't help it, though. It's like that thrum in his chest Stevie put there has only gotten louder, this steady beat between his ribcage, a song stuck in his head that he actually likes.

She's so easy to talk to. Like, regardless of the funky and completely out-of-tune jig she's got his heart doing, it's like there's no pressure, no expectations. Milo's used to nothing *but* the pressure and the expectations. They go hand-in-hand with even the vaguest of interest in someone, because eventually that someone wants something Milo doesn't, something he's not ready for.

And nobody ever gets that. It's this idea that *men have certain needs* and *all dudes want sex all the time*, and when Milo says he doesn't, everyone makes him feel like he's wrong, because *Of course you want to have sex, you're a* guy. There's a thousand ways to say the same thing, and every time it makes him feel like he's not normal. Like he's broken.

Because what else are you supposed to do with all that, when that's not how it is for you?

He'd been lucky, in a way, growing up in a small town and, by extension, going to a small high school. There weren't enough people around for casual dating. You were either coupled up or you weren't, and Milo wasn't the only person to fly solo. It was easy to keep his sexual preferences, or lack thereof, to himself.

Now, though? Not so much. It hardly got easier when he came out, either, because while he understood it for himself now, demisexuality is still this fairly unknown concept. And as much as Milo wants people to have the right idea about it, it's honestly so fucking *tiresome* to have to explain himself all the time.

Dating's just... hard. Sooner or later—and usually it's sooner, because *everyone is horny*, good God, how does anyone get anything done?—he has to admit that he's not into sex. Most people think it's some religious thing (he's *agnostic*), guys think he's closeted (not so much), and a lot of girls take it personally (which he gets, honestly, but he's not gonna give it up just to appease someone else's self-esteem, because what about his own self-esteem? Somebody's gonna lose, and Milo's always the one who winds up dumped, anyway).

It feels backwards to categorize it by gender like that, but there's something in the way people are socialized. Even Penn says they lean into traditionally feminine habits because that's all they knew in their formative years, and that shit sticks.

Funny thing is, if someone gave him *time*, Milo could be, y'know. *Down to clown.* It's just that he has to really get into somebody first, and *then* maybe he'll want to. But also maybe he wouldn't want to.

Yeah, he knows it's a gamble, and it's a waiting game before that; and he knows, even better, that nobody ever wants to *wait*. And after a while... Well. You just figure you're not worth waiting for.

Does he have to say that sucks? Because it really, really sucks.

He'd done this thing for a while, where he'd meet someone and immediately project his fantasies onto them. Maybe if he tricked himself into an emotional connection, then maybe for once he could be normal, maybe he could kick something off without it combusting within the same month.

This, unsurprisingly, did not work. It might have made things worse, even.

Milo really hates thinking about that, though. Because maybe all this *thinking* is only going to make things worse.

And, you know what, it's too early in the morning to be thinking about any of this, Milo decides, *resolutely*, while he sweeps the curb outside Nobody's.

Don't ask him why he has to sweep *the ground*, but somehow fuckin' Cooper always knows when he doesn't.

He tries to clear his mind as he finishes up the rest of opening shift duties, nukes a Hot Pocket in the stockroom (glorified walk-in closet) microwave, then does a lap around the store with a can of Lysol so it doesn't smell like Hot Pocket (ruins the ambiance), and clicks on the neon pink OPEN sign on his way back to the front.

He collapses in the chair behind the counter, buries his head in his arms, and groans for an obscene but necessary thirty straight seconds. No one comes in this early on Sundays, so he's got some time.

Or, no one but Penn Valerie, as it happens, when they breeze in at a cool 10:10 A.M. Penn's wearing their usual bed-head pixie cut, tortoiseshell glasses, the ugliest knitted poncho *in the world*, bike shorts, and the kind of sandals usually associated with Jesus and lesbians (a power duo if ever there was one), and a really, *really* obnoxious smile.

They also brought smoothies from next door, so, Milo supposes he can't complain. He does give them his best suspicious squint, though.

"You're not on the schedule 'til four. What do you want?"

"Wow. Okay. So the only reason I could bring you fruit smoothie sustenance is that I *want something* from you, and not out of the *goodness of my heart*?" Penn scoffs like they're actually offended, except they're *not*. "How dare you."

Right. Well, the thing is, Milo's known Penn since they were kids. They grew up next door to each other, got in the same trouble for doing cannonballs off the pool ladder and lighting unsupervised bottle rockets. They'd figured out their identities hunched in front of several open tabs on Google—demisexual for Milo, nonbinary and aromantic for Penn (they're still trying to decide on the sexual aspect of it all, but they're not too fussed about that part)—so. Point being, Milo knows when Penn's full of shit.

He tells them as much, even though he doesn't say much at all, just takes a pull from his smoothie straw and hums an unconvinced "Uh-huh."

"Well, fine." Penn throws up their hands, giving up the game because neither of them have ever been particularly good at lying.

(Hence all the trouble they used to get into, because honesty might be the best policy, but your parents don't actually give a shit about that when you admit to strapping Ken dolls to fireworks—even though, *in their defense*, they only did that when Barbie dumped Ken for Blaine the Australian boogie boarder, and they had to assume it was because Ken did something atrocious, so. *Whatever.*)

Penn props their elbows on the high-top counter, a simple feat since they're pretty tall, and admits, "Dottie told Artemis and me that you *serendipitously* ran into your future wife at Loretta's. And I was like, never been so bummed to be at an art show all week, I totally missed the intrigue, so, yeah, that's why I'm here."

"When did she tell you that? Did I miss the group chat?"

"You were—what'd she say?—*pointedly* left out of this one."

Sooner or later Milo's going to just start screaming. "Great."

Penn offers him an exaggerated pout, which does exactly nothing to help his mood. "Aaaaaalright, what's your problem?"

No sense in rehashing the details, since Penn got them from the rest of the peanut gallery. Milo presses the heels of his palms against his closed eyes. "I'm fucking... *confused*, man."

"Why? Because you met a cute girl?"

"Because I met a cute girl and I wanna *do something* about it."

"So?"

"*So?*" Milo drops his hands. "So I don't *do something*, Penn, that's not my thing. But now here I am, wanting to, and I just—I'm supposed to be—"

"No." Penn swipes a hand through the air, cutting his insecurities to ribbons. "Nope. I know what you're going to say, and you know what, kid?" (They've got all of two months on him, but okay.) "You're not *supposed to be* anything. You're still whoever you were a week ago. Sometimes there's just... an outlier."

This is another thing about Penn—aromantic as they are, they go bonkers for other people's romances. It's *fascinating*, they say, like they're living among some out-of-control social experiment. Milo's pretty sure Penn's got notebooks full of flow charts detailing the love lives of everyone in their acquaintance. Hell, they might have upgraded to a full-sized dry-erase board by now and he wouldn't be surprised.

"An outlier," he echoes dully. He'd thought the same thing, sure, but even still it's not sitting quite right—*but* maybe he only feels that way because it doesn't actually solve his problem.

He needs another Hot Pocket. Or maybe a lobotomy.

"*An outlier*," Penn repeats, with a little more *oomph*. "Me and Dottie talk about this all the time. Not in like, an official capacity, but when you're friends with a therapist, well, it's pretty much therapy pro bono, right?"

"*IIIIII* would not vouch for that."

"Well, okay, neither would I, but *anyway*..." Penn takes a bracing, kind of gross slurp from their smoothie. "Look, I get where you're coming from. Having a crush is, like, *unsettling* when that's not how you're hardwired. But d'you think, just *maaaaaybe*, you're overthinking it?"

"I *know* I'm overthinking it—"

"—love that self-awareness—"

"—I just don't know what I'm thinking *about*." He doesn't know, either, if that makes any sense.

"You're worried about the wrong thing," Penn says, like it makes perfect sense but he's still wrong. "About nothing, even. You're still demisexual, Milo."

Is he, though? Look, he knows he's been through this already—he hasn't *stopped* going through it, ever since Stevie walked into the store and made his brain go *brrrrrr*. Because that's the thing, is that his brain doesn't go *brrrrrr*! So now that it suddenly *does*, what does that mean for him?

He'd tried telling himself it meant nothing, that it didn't change anything, that he was being unreasonable or paranoid or *something* to think that a crush fundamentally changed who he is as a person. But he doesn't even know this girl; he didn't know her at all when this hit him the first time, and he only sort-of knows her now. How can he like her this much already?

He'd wanted to *kiss her*, the night he drove her home. He *would have* kissed her, if were any other guy—but that's the thing, is that he's never felt like *any other guy* before.

So it's just like... Now what?

"Alright," Milo concedes in the hopes that someone else will be able to tell him *now what*, "so what's the right thing to be worried about, then?"

Penn shrugs. "Nothing. I mean, nothing besides whatever it is people are usually worried about when they like someone."

"Liking someone's sort of my whole problem here."

"*Dude*. You're killing me. So you wanna take a cute girl to bone town, big deal. It's not like you woke up one day and wanted to fuck everything you could stick it in, just because it feels good. Which is dumb, right? I know we work here"—Penn gestures around the store—"and everything but, like, do people even have hobbies? Or do they just fuck around on their partners and pretend it's because it's in their biological nature?"

Milo's mouth twitches in bemused amusement (say that five times fast). "Which daytime drama have you been watching?"

"Just. So many, dude, the things the resident ex-boyfriend says are disgusto grosso. Like, it's never because they're polyamorous or something, it's always literally just because they're an asshole. They're all, oh, lemme blatantly disrespect my girlfriend because I saw another pair of tits. God. What *is* that? Never mind."

Penn waves a dismissive hand, a favorite habit shared with Artemis. "You're not *that guy*, is what I'm saying. *That* would be a problem. But this thing you've got going on? Not the disaster you think it is."

"But—"

"Nope." Penn points their jumbo straw, covered in oatmeal cookie smoothie, at him. "I've given this a lot of thought, okay? *Unobstructed* thought. Because I knew you'd be wiggin' out, meanwhile I am blessed with the third eye of an aromantic. Also, I smoked a *lot* of weed last weekend, mostly because I had to. It's the only way I can deal with the young people."

Today is not the day to deal with a not-even-midlife crisis. "You remember we're only thirty, right?"

"*Yes*," Penn assures him, "but we're young in that way where we're self-aware, so we know we don't know everything and we prefer it that way. We've seen enough. We don't want to know anything else. I'm talking about those young people who think the world is automatically going to be better once everyone who's over thirty drops dead. Meanwhile they'll all be indoctrinated into cults because they're so easily swayed by social media influencers, so you know what?"

Clearly, Penn's art show weekend was rattled by more wannabe social advocates who are actually less advocates, more assholes. They deal with this a lot. Milo knows the drill.

"I'd rather be dead," he supplies.

"Exactly."

"Carry on."

"Right, so, bearing all that in mind..." Penn shifts their shoulders back and forth, collecting their thoughts. "I think the thing is, *honestly*, Milo, I think we just feel so, like, *beholden* to our sexualities and our romantic predilections or whatever it is, because it's so...

"Not *unusual*," they decide, "but it's sure not normalized, either. So we feel this, like, *responsibility* to be the poster child for our shit. We have to do it by everyone else's understanding of what it means to be demisexual or aromantic or asexual anywhere along the spectrum. We have to be willing to disclose our personal thoughts and feelings to whoever wants to know at the drop of a hat, otherwise we're faking it, or we're not being a good role model."

"Does this have something to do with the young people?"

"Them and the weed, yeah," Penn admits. "Long story short, a bunch of us are out to drinks, we all get to talking, one of them gets all uppity with me because I should 'know better' than to be aromantic."

"Hey. Fuck them."

"I *know*. She seriously told me I'm sending the message that nonbinary people are inherently unfit for relationships. And it's like"—Penn digs the straw around their cup to disrupt the not-quite-crushed-enough ice—"my gender identity is non-binary, not 'a social justice stance.' But you can't make these people understand that. So why are we bothering to try being ourselves by anybody else's definition of what that should look like? Who *cares* what they think? Nine times outta ten, you don't even know them."

Except for the one time you *do* know them. That's the time that bugs him so much; that's the time that made Milo close up shop on his love life, and he doesn't feel any better about it now than he did back then.

That doesn't make Penn wrong, though—no, they're *right*, bar none. It's a little early in the morning to tackle his sense of self and all, but it's not like Milo wasn't already knee-deep in it before Penn showed up. He was already driving himself up the wall; they just found a way to make him sit still again.

Not that he's any closer to figuring this out, but he *does* feel better, so that's something.

"Anyway." Penn slurps smoothie off the straw. "Don't let the haters get you down, is what I'm saying."

"It's just weird," he says, because if nothing else it's still *that*. "I don't even know her and I feel like this. Meanwhile I know, like, you and Artemis, and I've never wanted to kiss either of you."

Penn waves that off, too. "You're a person, Milo, not a dictionary definition. Being demisexual doesn't mean you're attracted to *everyone* you have an emotional connection with. Especially you, kid, you have this way of finding your people and clicking. You met your roommate on *Tinder*."

"Who else was I gonna meet there?"

"A lot of people get murdered that way, probably. Isn't that what every SVU episode is about?"

"Maybe a couple."

"Well, the good news is Artemis won't murder you because he just won't feel like it," Penn says. "And Stevie doesn't come off as, like, particularly homicidal."

Milo knocks his forehead against the counter. "H*oooow* do I like her so much?"

"Right, I know it usually takes longer to forge a bond or whatever, but, I dunno. Maybe it's like I said, she's an outlier, or—call me a traitor to aromanticism," Penn offers, "but maybe this is a soulmate thing."

A *soulmate thing.* Yeah. That same, albeit errant, thought had occurred to him right off the hopelessly romantic bat, hadn't it? *Soulmates.* No pressure or anything.

"How high did you get this weekend?"

"None of your business. Excuse me for my passion. And you're over here meeting your soulmate, in which case..."

Penn hops on their sandaled feet, hazel eyes alight with that same schadenfreude-ish joy Milo's come to expect from his friends. "You've gotta tell me *all about* her. That's the best friend credo, dude. *Ride or die*, and we've been dead inside for *years*."

"Uh." Milo shakes his head into another pull of smoothie. "Wouldn't that suggest the ride is over, and now you need to mind your own business?"

"We've been over this, kid, my life is very peacefully without romantic intrigue. I have no business."

Yeah, Penn and Dottie are a real Shakespearean chorus in that way. Or a real Statler and Waldorf. Same thing, right?

"Gotta say, kinda surprised you don't know her already."

"I've seen her around, but c'mon, Milo, I'm back and forth between our *esteemed metropolis* even more than Dottie is."

True. Penn's very much involved in their whole art school grad scene, and lately they've been helping their cousin get his bar up and running, too. They haven't had time to hang around scoping out potential life mates for their oldest friend, or to set his spiraling ass straight when he goes into a panic about it. Those remain two of Penn's favorite hobbies, though, so it's no small wonder they're playing catch-up now.

"Yeah, I guess so," Milo agrees. "But do you—I dunno, do you maybe know anything about her?"

"Like what? Just ask her, doofus."

"But it's like—" He huffs. Under no circumstances does he want to talk about this, but he *needs to know*. "Did she ever go out with Erik?"

"*Erik* Erik? The guy who once asked a girl, right in her face, in public, 'What's cunnilingus?' Erik?"

Right. Milo remembers that. It was right here, in the middle of the store on a busy-as-it-gets Saturday night. How Erik picked up any girls after that well-publicized fact, Milo will never know.

"If I was gonna give you three guesses, yeah, pretty sure you just nailed 'em all."

"I mean, Erik gets around, so maybe?" Penn doesn't seem convinced, which isn't an indication of fact, but it does make Milo feel better. "I don't see it, though, and you *know* Artemis would've said something to you about it because he knows everything, so... tl;dr, I doubt it."

"Yeah. I don't know what I'm worried about, anyway. It's just Erik, it's not like he knows what he's doing."

It's a little, like, *absurd*, really, that Milo has more practical knowledge than someone with so much hands-on experience. But it's like he said before—it doesn't matter how much you've done; it matters how much you *listen*.

"I hate to say this"—but they're saying it, anyway—"and, yeah, that whole cunnilingus thing notwithstanding since it didn't harsh his moves, *somehow*, but Erik's like the smoothest guy on the planet. He's like a Kennedy. Or an eel."

"Why. Would you say this to me."

"It doesn't matter!" Penn says, in such a way that suggests it very much *does* matter. "We don't even know that they went out! They probably didn't! This might be wholly irrelevant! I just need you to be prepared for the possibility!"

"I've never been less prepared for anything in my entire life."

Penn's brow scrunches in thought, surely sifting through the catalog of stupid shit the two of them have done—including but not limited to that time Penn rode their bike down the big hill by the park, complete with Milo tied to the back of it and *on rollerblades*—but they come up empty. Because *even then*, they'd had the foresight to strap a helmet to Milo's head, knee- and shin-guards to his legs, couch cushions to his chest and back. But now?

Now, he might as well strip down to his Looney Tunes boxers and take a running leap off a cliff. At least this time he wouldn't ruin the family room furniture while he's at it.

"Not being prepared is better for this," Penn decides. "Like, fuck it. Get out of your head. Text her right now to see if she wants to hang out. For real this time, none of this professional sales associate bullshit."

"What should I—"

"Shut up! Who cares!" Penn's flailing their hands around again. "We've done enough deep-diving into our souls today! Stop thinking so much or you'll ruin everything!"

"Jesus, *okay*—"

They're right. Probably. Gotta be. Penn's never steered him wrong before—those couch cushions were their idea, after all—so Milo fishes his phone out of his pocket and shoots a text before he can (continue to) agonize over it.

Character development, here he comes.

ANATOMY OF A PORN TITLE

"**N**o, sir, I'm not even a little bit qualified to give you medical advice. If you're stuck in your penis pump, you *have to go* to the hospital."

Um. No way did she hear that correctly. The door to Nobody's settles in its frame and Stevie raises her eyebrows at Milo, behind the counter and on the phone. He raises his own right back at her.

He'd texted yesterday to ask if she wanted to hang out soon. If she hadn't been working, she would have shown up in the next fifteen minutes but, something-something capitalism, right? So he'd told her to come by today, which worked out since Tatum had plans with Whitney—gross, but it means Stevie got the car, so, fine.

(A whole-ass vehicle isn't exactly in Stevie's budget. She doesn't leave the house enough to justify the expense, either, but she chips in for gas and Tatum's cool with sharing.)

Stevie had started to dress carefully—*agonizingly*, some might say—the way you do when you want to look effortlessly desirable or whatever. But then, as she debated between shirts, she realized Milo wouldn't care, would he? Demisexuality considered, chances are he's not, like, an ass man or a tits man or a whatever-else-guys-are-into man.

She likes that possibility. It takes the pressure off. She doesn't have to try to *entice* him, she just has to be herself and that's enough to make him like her.

There might be a lesson in self-esteem happening here.

So she'd done her hair half-up, put on a flowy David Bowie tank, leggings, knockoff Birkenstocks a size too big because that's how she likes them, and she hadn't worried about whether she was too casual or sloppy, trying too hard or not trying enough. She did the same thing she would've done if she had plans with her friends, or if she didn't have plans at all. Being herself has gotten her this far with Milo, so, yeah. Maybe that's all she needs to do.

"Uh-huh. Well..." Milo's saying into the receiver, with the impressive restraint of a well-oiled customer service voice. "No, they see all sorts at the urgent care, this is small potatoes, sir... I can't speak to your policy, but emergency hospital visits are usually covered by insurance?... Nooo, we would not... Well, we don't manufacture the products, sir, once you have the instruction manual it's pretty much out of our hands..."

Stevie is trying very, very hard not to laugh. She clears her throat to shake off the giggles, and wrinkles her nose at Milo's know-it-all smirk. And then he has to go all toothy grin at her and—as is the custom with this guy—Stevie can't decide whether to be pleased or embarrassed. So instead she pretends to be engrossed with a *very* pink double-sided dildo that could, incidentally, double as a weapon; actually she's surprised that's not its God-given purpose.

"...I certainly can't stop you from trying to get out by any means necessary, just know that I don't endorse it."

Stevie has to slap her hands over her mouth to catch her laugh. The resultant snort isn't what she'd call attractive, but Milo's looking directly at her, *smirking* at her again, like he's daring her not to completely lose her mind. She's sure the man on the other end of the call can't hear her, though. She *hopes*. It sounds like he's having a bad enough day without some loser girl he doesn't even know laughing at his, uh, *plight*.

"...No, there is *genuinely* no need for a follow-up call, sir, best of luck to you... Yep. Buh-bye."

Milo clicks the phone into its cradle and Stevie bursts out laughing.

"In case you missed it..." He throws up unenthusiastic jazz hands and heaves a sigh, but it's clear he's trying not to laugh, too. "*Yeah.* That guy was stuck in his penis pump."

So, no, her Red Bull and iced honey bun breakfast didn't give her a sugar-induced hallucination, after all. Another giggle hiccups its way off Stevie's tongue, even as she scrambles for some *modicum* of human decency. "Oh, that's—no good."

Milo shakes his head. "No bueno."

"No diggity."

"No doubt." He clicks his tongue, tosses her a wink and another smile. "Not the first time I've heard that, though, we get at least two of 'em a year. Which isn't a lot, I guess. But."

"Weird that it happens more than once?"

"Right-o. *The problem*, of course"—and he sighs again—"is that these guys just keep pumping because they think it makes their dick bigger. Which it does? But only in the sense that, y'know, your dick's bigger when it gets hard. But *actually* these things work the same way Viagra does, it just gets the blood flow where it needs to be. And if the woebegone *assholes* who get stuck in it would just *read the instructions*, then they wouldn't have to ask me"—Milo throws his voice in what sounds like an impression of Yogi Bear, Stevie can only hope it's not on purpose—"'Can I use butter to get out?'"

"*Butter?*" Stevie repeats.

Milo flashes her the Girl Scout sign. "Hand to God, I could not make this shit up if I tried."

"This is *so* upsetting."

"Tell me about it." He hops out from behind the counter, sneakers squeaking when he lands in front of her. He gives her a big, goofy-around-the-edges grin. "Hi, by the way."

This time, when Stevie clears her throat, it's to disperse the butterflies trying to *strangle her*. "Hi. You look nice."

"Oh—thanks." He looks down, ears pink, at his short-sleeved button-down and cigarette jeans. "I try to, uh, class up the place with a nice floral print. Also we're supposed to lean more *business casual*."

"Do jeans count?"

"Well, just don't *tell on me*." Milo grins, stuffs his hands in his pockets and rocks on his heels. "So. We got a shipment of *two hundred* pornos this morning. Wanna make yourself useful, help me stock? I'll buy you lunch."

"*Make myself useful*," Stevie echoes. "You're kind of mean, you know that?"

"Right," Milo agrees, "that's why I'm buying your affection with takeout."

Okay, so, that's confirmation that he wants her affection *and* a promise of free food. Stevie's about to melt into a puddle at his feet.

There's a stack of boxes by the back wall, wire racks stocked with more DVDs than she would have expected, what with the age of internet porn and all.

When she mentions this, Milo slices the packaging with a box cutter and explains, "A lot of these guys—it's mostly guys—who buy porn are older dudes. Old habits die hard, I guess, and you get a lot of collectors in here, too. I don't know how much they even, ah, *partake* in their vast library of videos and skin mags because, as far as they've said to me, it's more like a comic book collection."

"That's... kind of interesting, actually."

"Yeah, for every dude who calls with a completely avoidable medical emergency, you get another one who could, like, teach a class on the history of sex media. And on *that* note..." Milo cuts the last box open with a flourish. "I'm about to be *very* immature about this. Go ahead, pick a card, any card, most of these titles are, in a word, *ghastly*."

Much to the disappointment of a few potential partners who didn't grasp the concept of bisexuality (in that it does not mean *sex addict*, which isn't something you should want, anyway? It's an *addiction*, not a kink. But. That's a train of thought to follow another day), Stevie's never watched porn. She likes a good erotic romance, but *watching* people get down on it has never been her thing. She'd love to say it's a moral dilemma about the exploitation of porn actresses, but the truth is she doesn't know enough about the industry to say. Maybe she'll ask Dottie about it sometime. Until then...

She unsticks a DVD from between the rest at random. The title's not as bad as she'd expected, but a little on the nose for her taste.

"Well?" Milo twirls a hand in invitation. "Let's hear it."

Stevie drops her voice in an approximation of a surfer stereotype (she winds up sounding like a Ninja Turtle, which, in terms of ruined childhoods, is only a *smidge* better than Milo's Yogi Bear). "*Soaking* WET."

"Nice one, Michelangelo," Milo congratulates her. "As for the title, no points for creativity."

"I'd give a couple for, I dunno. Biological accuracy?" Stevie skims the back of the box to make sure and, nailed it—"It's a squirting video."

Milo feigns a scandalized gasp as he ticks the title off his inventory sheet. "Oh my *stars*."

"This girl broke up with me once because I told her it's just pee. *Really*," she insists when Milo laughs. "She said I was kink-shaming her. But I wasn't, I swear, I just—she thought it was synonymous with, like, 'out-of-this-world big orgasm' or something, but it's—"

Aurgh. God. First of all, it's probably a safe bet to say that Milo knows what it is, considering where he works. He's got a handle on such themes and motifs as Misconceptions of Sexual Practices 101.

Second, perhaps most importantly, Stevie doesn't want to get into the *milieu* of it. The whole thing was that Kim wanted her to "Just try it!", as if Stevie has that kind of power over her body's involuntary impulses. Some people do, sure, but *some people* Stevie is not. Like, come on, she had a Red Bull and iced honey bun for breakfast, remember; she doesn't even have any basic willpower, let alone muscle control.

However. Regardless of the topics they've broached since the beginning, Stevie decides that she and Milo aren't quite *there* yet, so she moves on.

"I told her, sometimes orgasms cause bladder pressure and then, I mean..." She shrugs, and slots the DVD among similar titles on the shelf. "You're basically doing the same thing a seventy-two-ounce Slurpee does."

That gets her a full-body laugh. "*St*evie," Milo says, and her name drips with earnestness when he says it like that. "Are you tellin' me a seventy-two-ounce Slurpee gets your rocks off?"

"Are you tellin' me it *doesn't*?"

"Hey." He points his pen at her, a whisper of a threat more like *flirtation* than anything else. "What happens between me and 7-Eleven cherry limeade is no one else's business."

"You started it!"

"Uh, I believe that was *you*," he says, and points the pen at her with a little more showmanship, it almost flips right out of his hand, "when you kink-shamed a girl into breaking up with you."

Stevie knows he's teasing (*flirting*, but that makes her panic a little bit), but that doesn't stop her from getting all worked up. She's not holding a torch for Kim, *far* from it, but it was still, just, really fucking stupid.

"How much... *fluid*"—well, it's more delicate than *cum*, so that's something—"did she think our glands can hold? We're not a bottomless well of—of—"

"*Fluid*?" Milo supplies.

"Every synonym of ejaculate, *including* ejaculate, is worse than these porn titles," Stevie says, dead serious.

"That's the hill you wanna die on? Alright, baby face." Milo twirls his pen at the box, inviting her to pick another card, as it were. "Let's see where you're at by the time we're through here."

"Okay, but am I wrong? Genuinely, c'mon, tell me."

"Nah, you're totally right. The thing about the squirting, uh, *debacle*, too, is that in the movies"—he indicates the DVD she just put up—"when she climaxes, it's like this clear, uh, liquid. But that's because she's just, *bonkers* hydrated. We've got this regular who does porn, and she's got a friend who does the squirting stuff. She's on a diet of water for like three days before the shoot. I'm not sure if it's *just* water, that sounds dangerously unhealthy, but you get the gist."

"I don't think Kim watched porn. So I don't know where she got her ideas."

"Honestly I only know all the stuff I do because I work here," Milo admits. "But, yeah, I guess a lot of sex know-how is word of mouth. You know as much as you've heard, and half that's probably bullshit. Because, like, around these parts? Most of the people who talk about it are these guys who hook up a lot, so they're just bragging, but then they come in here and they say the most whacked-out shit you've ever heard. This other regular—uh."

Milo pauses, like he's trying to decide how much to tell her. Customer confidentiality, maybe? "Well, it took an *impressive* amount of time for me to convince him not to stick an anal vibe up a girl's vag. So. Do with that what you will."

Huh. That's either a coincidence, or it's definitely Erik. Madison had just texted Stevie the other day, all, *I don't know if this is like inappropriate and I'm sorry if it is but I'm just like ????? and*

you know him better than I do so maybe you've got some insight...
Blech. She already knows more than she wants to, so—

"I very firmly do not want to do anything with that," Stevie says, earning another laugh and a flush of pride in her chest (she's such an embarrassing simp for this guy, she wants to *die*; but then, it's not like cynicism ever did her any good, so might as well go all in).

Stevie unsticks another DVD. "*Breast Kept Secret. Oof,*" she says with nary a glance at the cover, because *nary's* all you need. "Misleading wordplay."

"Absolutely nothing secretive about breasts in that feature film, they're everywhere," Milo agrees with the utmost sense of put-upon professionalism. He checks the title off on his clipboard. "Also? Sounds like a pun a recipe blogger would make about chicken. One out of ten."

"We're rating by *ten?*"

"It sounds like a lot, I know, but trust me." Milo digs into another box. "You need all the variables you can get with this shit, like, here—*Look, Dad, I'm In Porn.* Why are you telling your father this?" He swipes the DVD through the air. "Negative ten thousand outta ten."

Stevie goes next. "*Bull for Hire.* Stupid title."

"But thankfully not an actual bull," Milo points out.

"Two out of ten."

"Respect." Milo checks it off and fishes for another. "*Cum With Me.* Blech, you're too right about synonyms for ejaculate. And, adding insult to emotional injury, this is just lazy."

"Slightly more, um. Interesting? If you say it in an ominous voice," Stevie suggests. She waves a hand to indicate the Tiffany playing on the company radio. "It kind of reminds me of, like, if you slowed down 'I Think We're Alone Now.' It's a certified banger—"

"—because it's on your playlist—"

"—but drag out the tempo," she reiterates, wrinkling her nose at Milo again for the call-out, "and you could totally get murdered to this song."

"Ah, I see your point. It's very new-millennia horror movie. But! On a related and yet *totally different* note—" His smile widens when Stevie laughs because, yeah, she veered them a bit off-topic. "*Cum With Me* isn't even good in its own right, so." He bobs his head thoughtfully. "Five and a half out of ten? For the potential. That sound fair?"

"Works for me. But, y'know." She drums her fingers along her jaw, all bullshit pensiveness. "Keep in mind, the Academy might have some thoughts."

"Ha ha." Milo marks the inventory sheet, then sticks the pen between his teeth. "Smartass."

"Pot, kettle."

"A true wonder we have any other friends."

They go on like this for a while—Stevie's not counting the minutes or anything, but it's long enough for her to think that Milo could have done this quicker without her. He never says a word about it, though, never *implies*, so as much as feeling like a burden is her natural inclination, Milo's not exacerbating it. It almost doesn't cross her mind at all.

That's new. She could get used to this. Maybe she already is. (And maybe that's all *too soon*, but, again she has to ask herself: what did cynicism ever give her?)

Stevie flips a DVD around to show Milo its fairly innocuous cover. "*We Live Together.*"

"Oh my God, they were *roommates*."

"Ten out of ten?"

"If you like that meme," Milo says, like he, personally, has had enough of it. "Otherwise? Three. It's like, sure, that's a popular trope, but why should we *care*? It'd be like calling a porn *Friends to Lovers*. I don't know these people, maybe their friendship sucks. Where's the context? The *plot*?"

"It's *porn*."

"I'm not here to judge one's medium of storytelling, Stevie, I just want it to be good."

If she keeps smiling like this, her face is going to stick. "You know, if any of your sarcasm was for real your actual opinion on something, you'd be the worst person in the world."

"*God*, could you imagine?"

Not really, even though she's the one who suggested it. He's too much like the best person in the world for Stevie to think of him as anything else. She can't keep going all starry-eyed at him, though, she doesn't want to freak him out, so! Next up—

"*Big Cocks*. Straight to the point." Stevie scans the back and makes a face. "Ew, wait, the blurb uses the word *turgid*."

Milo gags. "*Why* that?"

"I guess because it means 'swollen'?"

"It's technically correct but more importantly it's fucking heinous."

Stevie presses her lips together. Her face is warm with stupid, unabashed glee. "So what's the rating?"

"Nope." Milo shakes his head, knocks her arm insistently but gently with the clipboard. "Move along, I'm begging you."

Stevie does as he asks, and immediately regrets it. "Um."

"God damn it," Milo says when he pokes his head over her shoulder to look at the box. "*Poop Shooter Cuties*. Absolutely not. Negative."

"Negative what?"

"The biggest number you can imagine. I can't talk about this anymore, what's next?"

All too happy to oblige, she offers "*The Babysitter*. That was an urban legend, wasn't it? Possible copyright infringement."

"Mmmm, I don't know if that applies to urban legends, *your honor*. But I do know that you can't copyright a title."

"You're a bastion of knowledge, Milo," Stevie deadpans. He bows. "Either way. I guess after—jeez—*Poop Shooter Cuties*..." She trails off, enough said.

Milo nods. "The delicacy's appreciated. Four out of ten."

After that, there's *Bounce That Czech* ("Hilarious, but possibly culturally insensitive. Seven out of ten."); *Four Rooms* ("Looks like a classic romcom except it's all women. Ten out of ten, the lesbians win again."); *Little Oral Annie* ("Traumatized. Pretty sure this one isn't even a musical. Zero out of ten."); and—

"Oh, here it is, coming in for the *win*," Milo declares. "Besides the lesbians, I mean, but that's not really fair because no one else had a chance, but *anyway*..."

He flips the box a couple of times to set the anticipatory mood, then fully around to show Stevie the cover. "*He Came In My Hot Wife* 3. The *drama*, the *intrigue*, the *saga*."

"Eleven out of ten," Stevie decides. "I can't believe I have to hear about another Marvel movie every seventeen minutes when this is what franchises should be about."

"Right, I gave up like four Spider-Mans ago, I can't keep up." Milo nudges an empty box aside to make room for the next.

A quick glance tells Stevie that there are a lot of doubles of titles they've already stocked, and several more installments of *Poop Shooter Cuties* (no shade to anal sex, that *title* is just... unfortunate).

"Ah, damn it," Milo mutters when the bell above the door twinkles. Then he's all customer service. "What's up, Lars?"

"Not much, man. How's tricks?"

"Bitchin'."

Stevie shifts to Milo's other side. Nothing personal, but Lars has strolled over to the wall to peruse the DVDs and he's some guy she doesn't know, ergo she needs a good six feet of personal space to be comfortable.

He's exactly what she'd imagine of a guy named Lars: reedy, with a thin blonde mustache and unkempt scruff, a shirt with a tiger on it, ripped jeans and ragged cloth flip-flops. It's not that she has an *opinion* on any of those things—you just say *Lars* and, well, there he is.

Milo's rearranging shelves to make room for the new shipment. He passes Stevie stacks of DVDs, much appreciated as it gives her something to do with her hands; aside from the logistics, she thinks that's why he's doing it.

"Y'know, Milo, I've been thinkin'." Lars crosses his arms, squints at the titles on the *Ménage* shelf. "You know that place down the highway? 'Bout a half-hour drive, forty minutes. They got a theater, with the private booths, know what I mean? Y'all really need to get that here."

"We sell porn, man." Milo waves at the wall like he's Vanna White. "Don't you have a *home*?"

Lars snorts. "No respect for exhibitionism anymore."

"No there is *not*," Milo agrees. "Not when I'd have to mop up the stalls for ten bucks an hour."

"Speaking of," Lars goes on like Milo didn't say anything, "I'm seeing this new chick. You got any ideas where we can do it in public without it bein' illegal?"

Stevie covers her surprised laugh with a cough. Even Milo, who must hear stuff like this all the time, momentarily freezes in something like shock. He gives Stevie big eyes and she has to look away or else she'll lose it.

"What? No." He shakes it off. "For fuck's sake, Lars, stay away from the dog park and do cam work."

"'S not the same."

"Yeah, it sure isn't, 'cause cam work doesn't land you on the sex offender registry."

Lars hacks a derisive sound deep in his throat. "You know that thing's bullshit."

"*Sometimes.* Like, sure, you should be able to take a piss in the alley behind the bar, *if you must,*" Milo relents. "But I don't think you need to get freaky with somebody in the elementary school parking lot."

"I wouldn't do it there, I'm not a moron."

"This whole town is an elementary school parking lot. I mean like, metaphorically. You can't pull something like that. Just—I dunno, man," Milo gives up now. "Fuck with your curtains open, I think then it might be a property issue."

Lars perks up a bit. "Yeah?"

"*I don't know,* Lars, I'm not a *lawyer.*"

Another derisive snort or something like it. "Probably be doing better for yourself, if you were."

"Ah"—Milo places a solemn hand to his chest—"but then I never would have met *you*, and life would cease to have any meaning."

"You're such a dick," Lars says, with more mild amusement than heat. Milo blows a raspberry at him, and Stevie thinks, vaguely, about how he probably couldn't get away with that if he worked at Target.

His hopes duly dashed, Lars picks out a couple of DVDs—all of them exhibitionist to some degree, including *He Came In My Hot Wife* 3 (bless)—and follows Milo to the counter to check out.

When the front door shuts behind him, Milo releases a long, pained groan while he shakes himself around like he's expelling demons. "That—fucking—*guy!*"

Stevie tries for a sympathetic look, but it's useless. She's always halfway to giggling around this dude as it is, and after all that? She can't even try to stop it.

"Is that just, like, a day in the life for you?"

"Sometimes." Milo slumps over the counter, exhausted from his self-induced exorcism. "You get worse, and honestly a lot of times things are pretty normal. But when they're not, y'know, it's all..." He twirls a hand. "*That.*"

"And for all *that*," Stevie says, mimicking his disillusioned intonation, "do you really only get paid ten dollars an hour?"

"Eh. Fifteen," Milo amends. He props himself on an elbow to get a better look across the room at her. "But people like Lars think that's a livable wage, so then they go off about how we're *overpaid*. All I try to do is make sure this bozo doesn't pick up a criminal record, and he thinks I'm overpaid at ten bucks, even."

Oh, blech. Truly, Stevie doesn't know how he does it, nor does she have anything useful to say. So instead, she plucks another DVD from one of the leftover boxes.

"*Look, Dad, I'm In Porn Again.*"

Milo blows her a smacking, theatrical, exaggerated kiss. "Negative ten thousand *and one!*"

THE EPIC HIGHS AND LOWS OF GROCERY STORE MUSIC

M ilo is kneeling in his closet door with all the blind faith he can muster (how do Catholics live like this, *by the way*, he's already getting a cramp), surrounded by discarded clothes he continues to dig through, all the while lamenting the very real possibility that he has *nothing to wear*.

And upon *that* startling revelation, that's it, it's official: He's in his final countdown, the-world-is-ending overwrought teeny-bopper phase. It's gotta be something with the hormones that go, *so it would seem*, hand-in-hand with a crush. Teen angst has never felt more real—more *debilitating*—than it does right now.

He's *thirty years old*, he pays rent and usually makes his car payment on time, he eats reasonable servings of vegetables, he has two jobs—neither of which he has to work today *or* tomorrow, bless whatever good fortune allowed him something like a weekend after a record nineteen straight days (which is, in part, his own fault for picking up so many hours, but he still has lofty aspirations for a vacation, so here he is; but, *man*, fuck the "rise and grind").

Point is! He is as *fully adult* as it's possible to get—and yes, you can still be *fully adult* when your favorite pillow is a giant pig plushie, Milo will not under any circumstances betray Pigalatté on the off-chance that he'd make himself seem more arbitrarily *worldly*—and yet he can't even get himself *dressed.*

This is what happens when you like someone. When you lose your mind over someone. When you're so pent-up with feelings that have been otherwise foreign to you for so long that you're not sure you ever really felt them at all, not before *right now*, because if you'd *ever* felt like this before you would remember it with painful clarity.

Milo doesn't remember anything like this at all.

And he's almost normal about it by now, *almost.* It's more or less started to feel nothing but good, this thing with Stevie, but can you blame him if the frisson of underlying panic hasn't quite evaporated? He's very unpracticed and kind of scared, and he's got a handle on it, sure, but there's only so much he can control.

You'd think picking out a shirt would be one of those things, but—

"Should I wear this?" he asks, arms held aloft as he walks down the hall into the living room, and gives his roommate a spin for good measure. Not that a dime-a-dozen slim-fit gray tee warrants a spin, Milo's just trying to get his attention.

But Artemis, lounging on the couch, doesn't so much as glance away from the TV. "Oh, I'm not that kind of gay friend. You know this."

Milo drops his arms. "I've had to hear about Cooper's sports coat seventy *billion* times."

"That's a civil rights issue." Artemis does his signature hand twirl. "*You* can wear whatever you want. She's bi, right? Put on a Hawaiian shirt."

"Is that a thing?"

"Hell if I know, but it feels right."

Huh. Well, Milo has a grand total of three tropical print button-downs, so that's settled.

Stevie had texted this morning, telling him her grocery shopping was off so did he maybe want to hang out again? And *of course* he wants to hang out again; he's pretty sure he'd marry her if she asked him to (see? He's *so* normal about this). They'd made plans for later in the afternoon, and he's been just, totally wiggin' out over his wardrobe ever since.

With that all but sorted now, Milo lays on the floor to collect himself. "How was your lunch meeting?"

"You know me, there's nothing I yearn for like strategizing business card fonts at Chili's." Artemis turns down the volume on the baking show he's watching, Milo doesn't know which one it is, something about cupcakes. "Penn's cousin is a snack and a half, though, I don't think his bar needs advertising. We could just paint the downtown with his face and folks'll show up, they won't even care what it's for."

"I didn't figure Luca for your type."

"He's not, but he makes the boy band highlights work and I have to appreciate that skillset." He pauses to take a sip from his Arizona iced tea tallboy. "But, no, not all of us are looking to get swept off our feet," he adds, none too pointedly and with a smack of his lips.

Oh, here they go... Milo groans into the cradle of his arms. The floor smells like carpet cleaner. "I wasn't *looking*, it was an *accident*."

"You are so into this girl," Artemis says, as if this is news. He's usually more original than this.

"Yeah. I mean—*yeah*." No sense in denying it, might as well go for the full-body *yeah*. "Should I not be? Don't do this to me, man, I'm just getting used to it."

"I'm just surprised. You really peaced out after the whole Whitney fiasco."

"Okay, well—yeah." Milo doesn't want to talk about the whole Whitney fiasco. She's an asshole, end of, the rest of it he's quite happy to keep nice and repressed. "But this is... way different."

Artemis snorts. "No shit. Stevie's brain didn't atrophy at the age of thirteen-year-old mean girl, for one thing, and bless her for that. I just didn't expect you to jump in so..." He gestures with his tallboy. "*Unabashedly.*"

"It's been three years."

"I think time only heals all wounds if you deal with them first."

"I'm dealing, I've dealt, I'm fine." Milo rolls over onto his back. The ceiling fan whirs soothingly overhead. "I just—it feels different this time, anyway. I dunno, it's a gut thing."

The truth is, sure, Milo's been burned before, and *repeatedly*, and sometimes he does feel really jaded and hopeless about the whole thing. He'd more or less accepted that it might not happen for him, but even still...

There was always this shred of romanticism that he could never snap. It was a back-of-your-mind kind of thought, a *but what if?* that he could pretend wasn't there. But now that he has a reason to hope for something, the thought's been pretty much front and center. The initial—and *perfectly justifiable*, thanks—panic has mostly settled in a way that, again, Milo can handle. Things feel better than they feel bad, and isn't that something?

He's *trying*, okay, and that's more than he's wanted to do in a long time.

"Far be it from me to discourage you," Artemis says. "I give you shit, but you know I would *never*. I was just curious." He leans over to give Milo's face a hearty squeeze, the way your grandma does because you're just so cute or whatever. "Maybe a little worried about you, boo, if I'm totally honest."

"What for?" Milo asks, the words muffled with his cheeks squished together like that.

"You're a delicate flower." Artemis lets him go with a final pat. "Don't wanna see you get all busted up over somebody again. It's bad for your skin."

"Stevie's not like that."

"I didn't think so." Artemis lifts his iced tea in a cheers. "Glad for the confirmation, though."

"It's not like I got my heart broken last time, anyway. She just..." Milo trails off, unsure of how to explain what Whitney *just*. Because it wasn't about her, really, she could have been anybody; it was about the way she made him feel (which, in a word—a couple of words—*not good*).

"Yeah, I know. She *just*, and y'know I think that might be worse?" That doesn't really mean anything, and yet Milo knows exactly what he means.

"Anyway. Go on, get outta here." Artemis *shoos* at him. "Go getcha heart broken this time, or maybe have a little faith. Maybe swipe your V-card along the way. I've got our twelve dollars riding on it. See, because I have faith."

Milo groans, rolls off the floor and springs to his feet. Trips a little, very smooth. "S*top betting on my virginity, my life isn't a rejected John Hughes script."

"Oh, I *beg* to differ."

Right, that's a debate Milo's not into, for fear that his life is *precisely* a rejected John Hughes script and Artemis is about to give him a PowerPoint presentation as to the hows and whys. No thank you. His ego wouldn't survive that series of assuredly sick burns.

So before Artemis can decide to jump on that, Milo hightails it out of the room to go change his shirt.

***

Turns out, grocery shopping was only off because Tatum got called in to cover a yoga class, so Stevie's stranded with no car, no emotional support, and, ergo, no desire to brave the local Kroger.

Milo—ever the gentleman, thank you very much—offers to take her, and Stevie—ever the *Oh, you really don't need to do that*—tries to talk him down, so—again, *gentlemanly*—Milo has to practically frog-march her out of the house. Good thing she was already wearing shoes (bright yellow Crocs patterned with bumblebees. Between those and her ladybug tattoo, Milo's beginning to suspect he's lusting after a bug girl, which? That tracks).

"You could've given me a second to change," Stevie grumbles, even as she settles in her seat, criss-cross-applesauce, and dutifully clicks on her seatbelt.

Milo shoots her a quick once-over. She's wearing a KC & The Sunshine Band T-shirt with a hole in the collar, leggings with bleach stains around the knees. Her hair's up in a big swishy ponytail, cinched with a bright green scrunchie and a few bobby pins that aren't doing much for her flyaways. The stud in her nose is a little cubic zirconia butterfly (bug girl: Exhibit C).

"No way," he decides. He puts a hand on Stevie's headrest and then, while he's backing out of the driveway so he doesn't have to look at her—because what he's got to add is true, but he can't *look at her*—when he says, "Cute as a goddamn button."

"Don't patronize me."

He barks a laugh. "*Excuse me*, I'm all but worshiping the ground you walk on here."

"Is that what you call it?"

"That's exactly what I call it, yeah." Milo straightens, both hands on the wheel now, and cruises down the street. "So, obviously, we're walking that fine line between wife guy and 'If I can't have you, no one can' guy."

He can hear the smile in her voice, so maybe he's going overboard but if Stevie doesn't mind, neither does he. "No pressure, though."

"Oh, not a bit." He turns down a road that will take them through more of small-town Indiana's scenic empty lots, and points a finger out the windshield. "Hey, you think the 'Hell Is Real' sign counts as a roadside attraction?"

"Our greatest claim to fame," Stevie confirms. "What's that made of, do you think? Something indestructible, right?"

"Gotta be. I think it must be like, *one with the earth* by now, how else could it withstand the elements?"

"I guess we could Google it," she suggests halfheartedly. She crinkles her nose, scratches it with her thumb. "I don't think I want to know, though. Ruins the mystery."

"Good point, I want to live in ignorant bliss."

Milo searches for something else to talk about. He'd been at the duplex long enough to know it smelled like lemon Pledge and something orange, like maybe Stevie had plugged in an air freshener before Milo showed up. This possibility makes him *outrageously* pleased, because it's exactly the sort of thing he'd do if she were coming over to his place.

He'd gotten a look at the dry-erase house rules on the fridge, lending to several conversation starters, first and foremost—

"There is something oxymoronic about a straight boy rinsing his dishes," Milo says. "That's like... I dunno. Thirty percent why I couldn't live with my parents anymore, my dad left ketchup on everything. *Bless his heart.*"

"Well, you're demisexual, right? So that rule doesn't apply to you, anyway."

Ah. Welp. That's one way to get this conversation over and done with. Milo tries to keep the anxious butterflies from bursting in his gut. "Dottie, huh? She's such a snitch."

"I'm sorry," Stevie says, in that way where it sounds like she regretted saying something as soon as she did. "Was I not supposed to know?"

Milo shrugs. "It's not a secret. As long as you're, uh"—Jesus, here goes nothing—"cool with it, I guess."

"I, um. I mean..." She drums her palms against the insides of her thighs. They make a soft *pat-pat-pat-pat* sound, almost like rain against the hard-packed dirt of the backroads. "I like you just the way you are? So."

A lot of people think that at first, up until they realize how it affects their sex life. Milo doesn't say that, though. He's on the right track with Stevie—she's sweet in that quiet, nervous way, she's dry and funny and a little bit weird, she makes him feel like things could be *better*. They're onto something entirely better than he's had before, and he's got no reason to be defensive. He doesn't *want* to be defensive—he wants to be hopeful, open to the possibilities, he wants to be *vulnerable*, God damn it, and he wants that to be worth something.

So if Stevie tells him that she likes him just the way he is, he needs to believe that she means something by that, too. He *knows* she does, accounting for how goddamn *bashful* he gets when she says it.

He flips on the turn signal and checks out his window, a good excuse as any to look well and truly away. "Aw, *gawrsh*," he says, trying to laugh it off and it makes Stevie laugh, too.

"Butthead."

"*Butthead*," Milo echoes, aghast. "I *shudder*, *ma'am*, to think of what you'll call me once we've surpassed the introductory stage of our relationship."

"I usually call Tatum an asshole, but I think it's losing its shine."

"Gotta get creative with it. No holding back. Yadda yadda." Milo curls his hand into a fist. "Be like the two hundred pornos we stocked yesterday, Stevie. Be bold, be fearless, be—"

"Turgid?" She's way too pleased with herself for that one, Milo can hear it in her voice.

"Oh, ha, *ha*, *ha*." He smacks the steering wheel with each exaggerated *ha*. "You know I don't write the synopses, right?"

Stevie prods him in the arm, aka the greatest sexual thrill of his life. "You're the only reason I know about them. Guilty by association, *right*?"

"I don't know enough about the law to contest that."

He likes how much he can make her laugh. He's not even doing it on purpose, really, he's just saying the usual stupid shit he says; but it makes her laugh, so it doesn't seem all that stupid anymore.

So, yeah, Artemis was right again—Milo really is *so into* this girl.

(And, again—*obviously*. But, hey, it's nice to know that if Milo's in a panic spiral, he can easily bring his friends along for the ride. Solidarity.)

"Man, this place is a wasteland," Milo notes when he parks in the Kroger lot, where he counts a whopping four other cars.

"Yeah, late afternoon Tuesdays are always like this, that's why I, uh—that's why I always go out around this time." But Stevie's breath is coming a little short, like she took a steep flight of stairs too quickly. She sits up straighter, holds tight to her shins, and keeps talking.

"Because it's like, I need to get out of the house, right, but I need to have something to do, otherwise I'm just wandering around aimlessly and then that makes me nervous because, like, what am I doing, I probably look like I'm having a manic episode or something and it feels like everyone's looking at me, even though I don't think they really are but it *feels* like they are so I get all—all *flustered* and hot and like I'm probably going to cry myself into a panic attack even though I'm probably already having the panic attack, which shouldn't be embarrassing, it's not my fault, but then it's like, do I control my brain or does my brain control me, you know, and I don't—oh my God."

She tilts her head back, eyes closed, breathing deep with concentrated measures. "Sorry. I just—I'm sorry."

"Hey, it's okay." Milo clicks out of his seatbelt so he can face her fully. He doesn't know if she's having a panic attack right now, but it's at least panic attack-adjacent. "Can I do something? What do you need?"

"Just—a minute, I just need a minute." Stevie squeezes her eyes tighter, presses the heel of her hand to her forehead. "I'm sorry, this is…" She blows out a breath. "Embarrassing."

"Stevie, please. I routinely have to talk dudes out of their penis pumps, remember. Almost *literally nothing* registers as embarrassing after that."

He's not entirely sure if now is the time for jokes, but then her laugh comes shaky but genuine, so it can't be the *worst* thing.

"I just. Um." Stevie blinks her eyes open; they're a little brighter than usual. "I didn't think I was going to go out today, and then here I am, and I've never had you, like, um. *Chaperone* me before? So I'm worried about being a total basket case and then, just, the whole routine is just…" She slices a hand through the air. "*Kaput.*"

"Well, shit, sweetheart." Milo keeps his voice low, gentle, a little teasing. "This is what I get for dragging you out of the house. I should've asked better. I'm sorry."

"You didn't *drag me.*"

"There was a *hefty* handful of seconds there where your feet didn't touch the ground, I'm pretty sure."

Another laugh, easing back towards how it usually sounds (like she's always caught off-guard by it). Stevie wipes her eyes. "It's okay. I'll be fine, I just—should've let myself think about it more first."

Maybe so. But Milo's going to take some of the blame himself, too, and sort out a way to fix it.

So when they get inside and Stevie grabs a cart, Milo steps up behind her, puts his hands on either side of hers around the handle. She smells like that orange stuff in her duplex, and a little bit of coconut, like maybe she rubbed sunscreen into her cheeks.

Jesus. Okay. Milo *desperately* and dramatically wishes it wasn't such a challenge to not, under any circumstances, bury his face in her hair and *sniff her*, but apparently this is just who he is now. Talk about embarrassing. Also, unspeakable. Possibly liable for arrest. He tightens his hands around the cart to pull himself together.

Stevie cranes her neck to look at him. "What are you doing?"

"Making sure nobody infringes on your personal boundaries." Himself not included, clearly, but his intentions are entirely chivalrous. It's not like he's sniffing her on *purpose*. "You think it'll work?"

"I don't know. I've never had a human shield before."

"I am but a humble service dog to support you through your social anxiety." Milo taps his sandaled foot against her Croc'd one to get her walking. "That's why my parents named me *Milo*."

A grin kisses Stevie's mouth before she turns around, gets moving. "Is that a reference to something?"

"No, I just have a dog's name. I'm making it make sense."

The music on the store's speakers shifts from the fade-out of "Time After Time" to the more, ah, *boisterous* tune of "I Want It That Way." It's not Milo's usual Tommy James & the Shondells problem, but even so... *yeesh*. If he'd just broken up with someone, he would've turned on his heel right back out of the store by now.

Stevie must be thinking along the same lines. She sets a package of Milanos in the cart's baby seat and says, "Nothing like grocery store music to make you wanna lay on the floor and groan, huh?"

Funnily enough, Milo had been doing just that an hour ago. "You would know," he says, careful not to step on her heels as they walk. "Y'know I followed you on Spotify and all I got were more questions than answers."

"I'm an enigma," she says flatly. But when they turn down the next aisle, Milo catches the tail-end of another smile.

"You like *everything on the planet*." He nabs a box of pasta shells from the top shelf because Stevie can't reach. "And a few things I'm pretty sure aren't real. When do you have time to listen to it all?"

"Everything has its place." She squints at a display of tomato sauces and picks one that has a full serving of veggies in every half-cup (but how is that *earthly possible*, Milo wants to know). "Go ahead, name a band, genre, whatever, and I'll tell you when I listen to it."

Can't pass that up. First off, because he'll never get over it—electro swing: "Meal prep. I hate cooking, the music sucks me into a vortex of, just, a lot of *sound*. It makes the time go by faster."

Boy bands, including but not limited to the obvious (*NSYNC, the Backstreet Boys, One Direction, you get it) and then the not as obvious (LFO, LMNT, O-Town, and Hanson, all of whom are only not-as-obvious because people can be wildly uncultured): "The upbeat stuff when I'm getting ready to go out, the teen angst stuff when I've been dumped."

Country pop: "Only in the summer. It always feels sort of off to me when the weather's lousy."

Bruce Springsteen: "Always." (*Always.*)

Hip-hop, specifically '90s-early aughts: "Whenever I'm just bouncing around the house. There's usually day-drinking just to, um. Lower my inhibitions? So I really *believe* I can nail both parts of 'I Got A Man' by myself."

That playlist of songs she's pretty sure are about cunnilingus: "I'm not telling you what I use that for."

Milo scoffs through a smile he's trying to hide. "Don't tell me it's for something *nefarious*. You have *Tom Jones* on there."

"Yeah," Stevie says thoughtfully. The bags of tortilla chips in her hand crinkle as she places them in the cart. "In retrospect that one was a mistake."

"I don't know what you're talking about. Nothing sets the mood like 'What's New Pussycat?' W*hoa-oh-oh-oh—*"

Stevie spins around to slap her hands over his mouth before Milo can keep going. His surprised laughter bursts open against her palms.

"I'm deleting it. It's definitely not about sex, anyway—I don't think?" She wrinkles her nose, tilts her head in thought. "Or maybe it absolutely is. I don't know, it's debatable. But it was funny at the time."

She drops her hands, wipes them on Milo's shirt while she's at it. "And what time was that?"

"Half-off margarita Wednesday."

"*Lush.* Okay, how about..." Milo hums as they turn into the freezer section. "Disco. More disco than belongs on this side of the 1970s."

"Hey. I like disco."

"*Clearly.*"

"Oh, I'm about to make you feel so bad about yourself—"

"—joke's on you, I already hate my guts—"

"—disco got popular because queer people liked it," Stevie soldiers on. The only indication that she heard his smartass remark is the elbow she digs into his side. "It was *fun*. Our bars and clubs put it on the map. And the *fashion*, jeez, it was bright and kooky and—*flamboyant*, you know? It made it okay for us to be ourselves, because it made us a part of something that wasn't just ours, like—"

She flaps her hands, much like she did during her breakdown of *The Little Mermaid*. "There were no lines between us and them anymore, right, because this was *music* and *pop culture*, we affected musical revolution, because we actually had a say in this entire other subculture that turned into something bigger. And, fine, so you could say a lot about the drugs and the, um, unsafe promiscuity, I guess? That was part of the subculture, too, but then you'd have to criticize rock for the same thing. And I'd argue—lots of people would, I think—that rock was more about... *masculinity*? Just fully hetero male sexuality. But the sexual liberation of disco was for everyone."

Well. Shit.

There are a dozen things there that could be Milo's take-away, *should be* his takeaway, but he must be having a weirdo self-esteem day because what he lands on is an admittedly uncharitable *maybe not for* everyone.

Not that that negates Stevie's point, but Milo's definitely never felt *liberated*—comfortable in his own skin most of the time, sure, but... It's not the same thing. These movements and revolutions are never for people like him. He's always right there on the outskirts and—and, fine, so he's being entirely selfish here but, look, this is just making him feel some kind of way.

Some kind of way that he can examine later; he's not about to have a full emotional breakdown in the frozen food aisle (been there, done that, can't make it a habit). If he ever achieves self-actualization during "The Hustle," he'll owe Stevie, say, nine thousand dollars.

Anyway, he gets what she's saying. There's so much more to disco than whatever some wannabe music snob would let you believe. It's *important*, regardless of whatever his problem is right now. Condemning it for being cheesy or just plain bad or whatever other condescending thing you can dream up is *missing the point*, so—

"You're right," Milo sighs, "I'm an asshole. Also? I'm obsessed with you."

That gets him another elbow. He fakes a dramatic wheeze Stevie doesn't buy for a second.

"Throw Wikipedia a donation. Seriously, I'm—it's no big deal, knowing all that," she says dismissively, bashful the way she makes Milo feel. "I like something, I look it up so I know more about it. That's all."

"Sorry, but it's still, uh, really fuckin' cool."

"Please, stop, my ego can't take it."

"Gettin' too big for its britches, huh?"

"About to bust the zipper and everything." Stevie lifts one of his arms, walks beneath it to get to the frozen breakfast foods a couple displays away.

It figures that, as soon as Milo dead-set resolves not to have some kind of episode (breakdown? Only time will tell) in full view of the Toaster Strudels, the all-too-familiar strings of "Crimson and Clover" strum their way over the speakers.

Isn't. That. Just. *Hilarious.*

"Oh, here! We! Go!" Milo accompanies each word with a stomp of his foot, sandals slapping enthusiastically against the speckled linoleum. He windmills an arm, too. "*God*, Stevie, I know you know this one," he says, snapping his fingers in quick succession and completely out of tune. "It ruins my life every time I'm scrounging for sales on Bagel Bites."

"Sure, I think this one probably haunts the dreams of every hot young single in your area," Stevie agrees. She's making fun of him a little bit, Milo can tell, but she still agrees with him. That's self-awareness, baby. "I am a little worried you're gonna maybe punch yourself in the face, though?"

Milo puts a conscious effort into slowing down the windmill. "I'm just trying to... I dunno. Expel my inner demons without bursting into tears in front of the, uh..." He squints at the freezer display next to him. "Meat substitutes. Huh. You think there's any porn that plays on that?"

"Well, sure, you've got a whole vegan audience to appeal to," she says, like they've got a pitch meeting coming up. "And the pun's right there. Somewhere."

"Yeah, there's something here about *corning the cob.*"

A pause. Then, "I. *Desperately.* Want to argue against that."

Milo grins. "But you can't."

"But I *can't.*" This is paired with a pitiful and yet devastatingly cute whimper. "I don't want to talk about this anymore," Stevie decides on a defeated laugh, promptly swallowed by a puff of cold air when she opens the door to the waffles.

And, you know, all of a sudden (and yet not at all unexpected), Milo feels like an idiot. Not in a bad way; but in that lovesick kind of way that makes you reevaluate everything you ever thought you knew about what it'd be like to fall in love.

(And, no, "Crimson and Clover" is—*as per ush*—not helping in any way shape or form. *But!*)

(...He's not sure what the *But!* is, exactly, only that there is one.)

The truth is, he never knew what it would be like. He'd fantasized, sure, had thoughts and feelings and *hopes*—that was always the hardest thing, the *hopes*, those were the things you had to let go of sooner or later, because sometimes you hoped too much, and you'd only end up disappointed when they didn't follow through, but— (Always a *but*.)

Now the music's getting to him, maybe. Or maybe this is The Moment where everything *clicks*, it all falls into place and you realize some life-altering truth about yourself that fixes everything with just the *thought* of it—and you can't have The Moment without the music, right?

For as much as he'd never *known*, right now and all of a sudden, Milo can't remember what the *not knowing* was like. Because—and, Jesus, he can hardly believe this is happening for him, he really is going to lose his mind next to the meat substitutes—*right now*, every doubt has been stripped away so soundly it's like he never had a reason to doubt at all. It feels out-of-nowhere and simultaneously like he should have seen it coming this whole time.

Stevie balances two boxes of waffles in one hand, shuts the freezer door with the other, and at the same time she opens a whole new one.

He's probably overusing metaphors (or whatever!) here, but Milo is way too head-over-heels—and very possibly head-up-his-ass—to care.

"But just, in the name of... *wooing*," Stevie's saying, as she dumps her waffles into the cart and remains oblivious to the white noise crazy going on in Milo's head, "can I give you some advice, and it's advice I have no real business giving, but I'd be, um, *remiss*, to leave you hanging, so—"

She huffs, loose tendrils of hair fluttering, and goes back to the freezers—sausage biscuits this time—as she keeps talking. "I don't think *corning the cob* is anatomically correct? I mean, I don't know, something's lost in translation there, and also I think we've just, like, totally lost the plot of this song."

"Yeah." Milo has to agree with that; this conversation has really gotten away from him. He elbows the door closed before Stevie can price-compare her breakfast sandwiches. "Hey, can I kiss you?"

She blinks. Her hand twitches in mid-air, frozen in time at the door handle. Another blink, and then she looks at him with eyes wide enough you'd think she'd never blinked a second in her life. "I don't understand the question."

"I could not *possibly* make it any clearer."

"You could've just gone ahead and done it."

"That seems... rude."

"Well, ah. Um. *As it stands*, I have zero breakfast sandwiches and also no kisses, so..." Stevie lifts her hands, palms up, and shuffles around as if redistributing the weight between her options. "You tell me what's rude. Or—wait, shoot—"

Her words are coming so quickly she's tripping over them. "*Oh*, that was supposed to be smooth, I think? But I don't think it worked, it definitely didn't, I—"

"Nah." Milo waves off the apology before she can finish it and then, before he can second-guess it, he's got his hands on her face. "I think it worked."

She tastes like beeswax lip balm, right before he kisses her.

And when he *does* kiss her... He can't register what she tastes like, just the way she makes him feel.

Because what he feels is the twitch of her lips, and the surprised laugh she breathes past his. He feels the clench of her grip at his waist—the slightest bit cold, residual frost from her chocolate chip Eggos—and the pinch of her chipped-paint fingernails that sends his blood shooting in all kinds and sorts of directions that cannot be medically advisable (your blood probably shouldn't be *shooting*, right? Certainly not in loop-the-loops). He feels the slip of her tongue that makes his heart slip up, ricocheting back and forth on a banana peel he never knew was there.

He's all nerves and possibility, nerves and *relief* that she's just as keyed-up as he is—because he can feel that, too, in the accidental nip of her teeth and the *Sorry, I'm sorry*, the breathy giggle he gets in exchange for his smile, and he eats it all up with the insistent (*clumsy*, whoops) stroke of his tongue.

He's all *more more more*, all at once, right off the bat he can't get enough of her—because she's all he's ever wanted, he can feel that, too, and there's no getting enough of that, is there?

Definitely not.

For someone who didn't know a whole lot of things up until now, Milo sure is catching on quick.

She tugs him a little closer, and he *goes*—one hand cupping the back of her neck now, careful not to mess up her hair. He's hell-bent focused on following the rhythm of her mouth, on not bumping her nose or using too much tongue in his unpracticed eagerness.

What can he say, he doesn't get out much. He can catch on to the feelings part of it, no problem; technique is a whole other animal.

But it's like he couldn't mess this up even if he tried. Because this feels so *right*, and he's never felt right like this before. He's never felt like he fits, not the way he fits with Stevie.

She plays along with his jokes and worries about whether he's safe to drive, she doesn't want to bother him but *all he wants* is for her to blow up his phone like a spambot, and all the while—here's the important part, the kicker—she's giving him the crazy-good butterflies you get when you know something good's coming.

She lets him kiss her smack in the middle of the grocery store, and she kisses him back like she knows how much it matters, because maybe it matters to her just the same.

You never know what it's going to be like, when you fall in love. It seems like it's going to be fireworks and forever and like nothing's ever going to hurt you again, and maybe that's true—but then, it's not as big a *to-do* as all that. What Milo knows for sure is that it *happens*, and you don't need any more promises than that, because the happening's enough.

If you asked him how he knows, he couldn't tell you. It's like he said to Artemis—it's a gut thing. And if you asked him something like, *Hey, isn't it too soon to know? Or for 'gut things'?*, he'd say who cares, it's not like you can stop a feeling.

He kissed Stevie because he *wanted to*. He's still kissing her for that same reason, and also because she's kissing him back like she wants to keep it up, too. Kissing—the concept, the act itself—was never going to change his life, he always knew that. But kissing Stevie?

Jeez. Us.

Milo's breath catches, and he lets it go into another kiss as the instrumental winds down over the speakers above them (around them, inside them). That's sure worth reevaluating it.

KISSING MONTAGE INTERRUPTUS

DOTTIE: In the GROCERY STORE. Really?

MILO: there are six ppl in this chat, who are u talking to

DOTTIE: Don't play coy.

MILO: *typing...*

STEVIE: *typing...*

ARTEMIS: *typing...*

PENN: *typing...*

TATUM: *typing...*

ARTEMIS: They did WHAT in the grocery store?????

TATUM: Something the clementines will never forget

PENN: O.O

STEVIE: ??? i didn't even buy clementines

TATUM: No duh, they all withered away after you went and did it right in front of them

MILO: christ alive DON'T say it like that

ARTEMIS: **DID IT**?????

MILO: see now look what you did

ARTEMIS: WHERE is that gif of Blanche spritzing herself with the water bottle when I need it!!!!!

MILO: BLOCKED.

STEVIE: what did *i* do???

MILO: EXCEPT FOR YOU
u come with me

ARTEMIS: :') They grow up so fast

MILO: dottie if u were my therapist i'd fire you on the grounds of BETRAYAL

DOTTIE: Too bad we're just friends. That's forever, bby. <3

MILO: WE'LL SEE

PENN: *edited the group chat name to* THE DRAMA LLAMA EXPERIENCE*

TATUM: Love that. Sounds like a band.

ARTEMIS: Rock 'n' roll, my little honey nut queerios
Even if you gotta do it in the KROGER

***

MILO: i really seriously am not speaking to them ever again this time, i mean it

STEVIE: well don't sign it in blood or anything

MILO: TOO LATE

STEVIE: ... :|
the drama llama experience deserves their own vh1 special already

MILO: fr the music industry's never seen a fallout like this!!!

STEVIE: fleetwood mac, eat your heart out

***

As much as Stevie's dated—which isn't *much*, really, but enough that you'd think she'd know by now—she never knew what it felt like to be on cloud nine, so to speak.

She was so used to things fizzling out in an entirely anticlimactic fashion, occasionally with a little more pizzazz but then she felt like shit about herself, but either way she was never *quite* walking on sunshine (Katrina & the Waves), dancing on the ceiling (Lionel Richie), caught up in you (38 Special), whatever, it never hit her like this.

But now she's got *this*, and she's doing all of the above.

Not that she's going to say that out loud or anything—feelings are embarrassing—but Stevie takes comfort in the fact that this is *it*, he's her person, he's the ever-evasive The One. She can't even feel stupid about thinking so, it feels so right.

Milo has become, in strangely (but at the same time *assuredly* and *rightly*) short order, the person who takes all of her in exchange for all of him. Right from the jump he fit into all her empty spaces and, all considered, Stevie must fit into all of his, too. They *click*, they work, and maybe it's too soon to say so? But it doesn't feel too soon, it feels like... *well, duh.*

She thinks that's probably how it's supposed to feel. When you know, you know; what else is there to do?

Sometimes she goes to see him at work, when she has Tatum's car and a completed (or near enough) to-do list, and she's not in one of those moods where she thinks she's the most annoying person on the planet. But Milo never makes her feel that way. He always wants her around, always happy to see her when she strolls through Nobody's door, and that's helped to ease her anxiety.

She might think it's just because she brings him snacks, but one time she made a not-really-a-joke joke about it, and Milo said, mid-sip from the soda she got him, "You brought snacks?" And he'd smiled so big when Stevie laughed, she has to believe that *that's* all he really wants.

When they're at his place, they watch TV in his room because it's the coldest one in the apartment and Stevie likes a chill. It's not a move to get cuddles, but she gets them, anyway. Dottie called Milo a worm on a string, but Stevie would call him more like a stuffed animal that came to life, he likes to cuddle with her so much.

Usually Artemis will wander in and crawl between them on the bed, groaning about a difficult client or the line at UPS, or that the McDonald's ice cream machine was down again and that if he doesn't find a way to get a McFlurry, he *will* kill someone.

(That time, Milo Doordash'd the McDonald's an extra five minutes away, whose machine was blessedly in order, because "Even outrageous delivery fees are a *small price* to pay for my *life*.")

They listen to music and Stevie talks his ear off with little facts and figures while they paint each other's nails; she's partial to any shade of blue, and Milo always goes for whatever has the most sparkle. So far his favorite playlist of hers is a tie between *bangers* ("This baby can fit so much *versatility* in it!") and *portrait of an existential crisis* (they lay on the floor and *ponder* to this one a lot).

They sleep in each other's beds—yes, actual *sleeping*—and they pretend not to know that they take it in turns to sneak out in the morning to brush their teeth. And they pretend, too, that they both wake up smelling like spearmint, and they giggle stupidly, uncontrollably, because it's bullshit and they know that they both know it.

And sometimes—oh, *sometimes* (dreamy sighs and all)—they kiss, and it's the kind of kissing that makes Stevie believe that maybe Disney movies got a few things right, after all.

The first time Milo kissed her, Stevie was thrown off-guard. Not in a bad way, just in a seriously-for-real unexpected way. Who *expects* the guy of their dreams to lay one on them in the middle of boring errands, *and* in the midst of a conversation that had gotten wildly away from them both?

It had been the last thing on Stevie's mind, so much so that it hadn't even teased the fringes of her thought process, like, we're talking *zero* disruptive thoughts here. Zero thoughts, period, even.

But when Milo kissed her... Look, she doesn't say this lightly, but—*va va voom*, you know?

She hadn't thought he'd make the first move. But he did, no holds barred, and that feels like a good sign.

They've kissed plenty since then—quick kisses, *languorous* ones, ones that toy with the idea of getting hot and heavy without ever quite getting there (not yet, anyway). There's a decided lack of expectation that makes the kissing that much *better*, because it doesn't have to go anywhere else. Kissing gets to be its own thing without either of them leaving disappointed because "That's it?", because it's not *it*, it's just enough all on its own.

He doesn't touch her like he likes it, exactly—more like he's figuring out *how* to like it, the *why* of it and what he's supposed to do with that, and what the right way to do all that is.

That's what Stevie figures, anyway, because the way Milo touches her, kisses her, tends towards the slow, tentative, he hovers a lot.

It doesn't bother her. She thinks she gets enough about the demisexual thing to assume that this is normal, just something he needs to get used to before he's comfortable. She's gone through dry spells before that make her kinda rusty with everything, too, so maybe it's like that.

Whatever it is, Stevie's not in any rush. She'd rather go slow with someone she likes than get off on some one-night stand with someone she doesn't want to listen to talk, you know?

Besides, the slower they go, the longer she doesn't have to introduce him to her parents. Her mom and stepdad will like Milo just fine—better than fine, even! They'll probably love him!—Stevie's just... not big on sharing her romantic life with them. Leave it at that.

Anyway, it's nice, too, to marathon SVU without someone trying to feel you up when you very seriously just want to watch TV. Milo's too busy pitching ideas for his spin-off series (ADA Barba and Dr. Huang as a crime-fighting duo whose weapon of choice is sick burns, in SKU: Short Kings Unit) to cop a feel. Occasionally, mid-sentence and mid-hand gesture, he'll lean forward to kiss her on the nose while he's still talking. It's casual, absentminded, dripping with affection. Stevie likes that *infinitely* better.

For once sex isn't the goal, the high point, the endgame—it's just something that might happen later down the line. Until then, Stevie doesn't have to worry about it when she shaves and inevitably misses that entire spot behind her knee (seriously, *every time*).

Things are good. And there's no pressure for them to be anything other than that.

***

"Sheeeeeezus. *Finally.*" Stevie skims the email one more time to make sure, then shuts down her laptop before anyone else can tell her there's a problem; it's in God's hands now.

"All done?" Milo asks from his seat in the big recliner. He waggles his socked feet at her.

(He'd shown up in socks and slides, *the* fashion faux pas, because he only wears real shoes when he has to but he says the duplex is *frigid.* Stevie argues that sixty-seven degrees is *comfortable*, thanks; Milo calls her unreasonable and keeps his socks on. These ones have Mr. Bighead on them.)

"Yeah, and right before I fully lost my mind, too." She clicks the laptop shut, shoves it away, and promptly crumples to the floor. "It would be. *Great.* If the publisher *told me* there was an extra chapter added, so I'd know the cover dimensions they sent me the first time were wrong."

"*Oof.*"

"It was *thirty-seven pages.* Did they really think that wasn't going to change things?"

"Well, that's what you get for including 'mind-reader' on your resumé." Milo pats the arm of the chair. "Let's go, get over here and I'll squeeze the agitation out of your body."

Stevie pushes herself off the floor and climbs into the chair next to him. It's big enough that they don't need to overlap too much, but they tangle their legs together, anyway. And, as promised, Milo loops his arms around her and *squeezes* like she's a stubborn bottle of toothpaste that might as well be empty, but he's even more stubbornly determined to get his money's worth.

He's in faded jeans and a shirt with the sleeves cut off, so Stevie has an unobstructed view of the tattoo on his arm. She's seen it countless times now, but she's never asked about those flowers she couldn't name.

She traces the thick petals, down to the stem of one of the leaves. "What's your tattoo for?"

"Honestly?" Milo shrugs, gaze tracking her movements. "I just thought it looked cool. A guy at the auto shop does tattoos, too, and he's got, like, an especial knack for plants and stuff."

She taps a petal. "What kind of flowers are these?"

"Marigolds. I'm an October baby. And the lyrics"—he twists his arm so she can see them—"are Springsteen." He half-sings them. "Obviously."

A smile touches her mouth. "Obviously."

He curls a hand around her wrist and pets her ladybug. "What about yours?"

She shrugs, too. "Good luck. I'm so nervous all the time, I figured I could use it."

"Hm." Milo presses his lips to it, slow and easy. He runs his other hand up her thigh, fingers tapping out the pattern between her beauty marks. It makes her feel all wriggly. "That publisher didn't get the memo, I guess."

Stevie groans, laughs. "Tell me about it."

"Well, back in my day, we had to walk *fifteen miles*, uphill both ways, in the *snow*, with *no shoes*, to get the mail, only for the publisher to not tell us they added twenty pages—*mmph!*" Milo's laugh gets caught in the pillow Stevie smacks in his face.

"Ah." He grabs it, tosses it onto the couch with a soft *fwump!* "I like you."

She sticks her tongue out at him. "I like you, too."

And she does. A lot. So much that she's not sure where to put it all.

Stevie can't make herself feel stupid for falling so head-first into this thing with Milo—she wouldn't want to, either—but she is still trying to figure it out. It's not that she wants to question it, but she wants to understand it, so that her usually-dominant logic can catch up to the way she feels.

And the thing is, she's comfortable with Milo in a way she'd always wanted but couldn't fathom was real. It was just so unattainable. Every failed relationship, every conversation that never went anywhere else, anywhere *real*, never felt like it was bringing her closer to what she wanted; it just felt like a disappointment. It felt like... How long was she supposed to do this before she just gave up? How many times did things not work out before you found the one that did?

That's all very grizzled and jaded for a twenty-four-year-old, she knows. She's barely had a life yet, she shouldn't complain, blah blah, she had plenty of time; it's just that she was tired of wasting it.

Milo's not a waste. Milo makes it all seem worth it, like it doesn't even matter because she doesn't have to do all that anymore. It's like... *Goooooodbye*, unsolicited dick pics. If that's not a reason to fall in love, *what is*?

(It's more than that. *Obviously*, Stevie would hope. But sometimes you have to distill it down to one thing, and she thinks that one pretty much encapsulates everything she can't otherwise put words to.)

She scrubs her fingers through the slight stubble along Milo's jaw. "You're so pretty."

He tries to laugh it off—he always does, when Stevie goes all moony-eyed at him. It might make her self-conscious, but she thinks he only does it because *he* is. "Ah, shucks."

"*Really.*"

"Even my crooked eye?" he hedges. "Not that I'm like, at all self-conscious about it or anything," he adds, clearing his throat in a way that suggests he very much is, actually.

It puts Stevie somewhere between sad and angry on his behalf. From her experience, she never had reasons to feel bad about herself until other people started pointing them out. She can't imagine what it's like to deal with that when it's a disability, but the mere notion has to be enough to piss anyone off.

"I like it. Not in a, um. Fetish way?" Ugh, this isn't coming out right. "I just like..." She gestures to and fro. "Everything you've got going on here."

"*Flatterer,*" he teases, but the tips of his ears are red with sincerity. His hand flexes around her hip. "Keep sweet-talking me like that, I'll start making out with you and *never stop.*"

"Don't threaten me with a good time."

"You *would* think that's a good time." Milo snorts at her. "Harlot."

She pokes him in the stomach, feels it flex. "What. *Ever.* You talk up butt plugs for a living."

"*Ha.* That's a civil service. Otherwise the hospitals would be overrun with people who take the jumbo plug up an ass that's never even seen a prostate exam."

Stevie blinks at him. "Somehow I still want to make out with you."

He seems a little surprised, then pleased with her reaction. "Thanks. It's my natural animal magnetism."

"That sounds inconvenient for a demisexual."

"Well, it only works on funky little bug girls who've got a birth mark right—here." Milo ducks to kiss the mark in the hollow behind her left ear. He keeps his lips there when he says, "So I think I'm doing pretty okay for myself."

"*Pretty okay.* Sure, and *I'm* the flatterer." Stevie rolls her eyes, then tips Milo's smile to her own so she can proceed to kiss his face off.

He tastes like Mountain Dew, rainbow sour strips, and waxy original ChapStick, inspiring sense memories of the first boy Stevie kissed sophomore year of high school. It makes her huff a laugh against his mouth; Milo's lips part to catch it.

"You're gonna give me some kind of complex," he murmurs, but she can feel his smile.

"You taste like—like an inadvisable sugar content." And she's got a sweet tooth, so she kisses him a little harder for it. His ever-present laughter makes him taste all the better. Makes Stevie *feel* better, too.

He makes her feel all melty like hot fudge sundae syrup, her body tingle like her nerves are made of Pop Rocks. She's just... *jittery* whenever they kiss, like Milo's a personified sugar rush and Stevie has no willpower so she's going to gorge herself until she crashes.

Or not quite, because—

"Oh! Hang on." Milo's hand flexes around her hip, his fingers drumming excitedly. He gives her one more smacking peck before he unsticks their lips. "I made you something."

He shifts to get his phone out of his pocket, taps the screen a couple times and then shows it to her. It's a Spotify playlist—*kissing songs for my main squeeze.*

"*Oh*, wow." Stevie nabs the phone, scrolls through it (Patti Scialfa, Boyz II Men, Hozier, Frankie Valli and the Four Seasons, the list goes on in deliciously varying fashion). "That's romantic."

"Well, sometimes. But I, uh. Got a little carried away," he admits, sheepish and joking all at once. "Like imagine we're going at it and then 'Go Go Power Rangers' starts playing."

Stevie's pretty sure her laughter physically jostles the chair. "*Why* is that on here?"

"*Mi amor.* Hello. It's a *hype song*," Milo explains. "I gotta keep my confidence up. If it kills the mood, well, *so be it.*"

"I guess we'll see how it goes." Stevie hits shuffle and tosses the phone over to the couch. They start off with The Pointer Sisters' cover of "Fire," so they're starting off strong.

And she's buzzing, popping, melting all over again.

Stevie knows because he told her, that Milo's only ever kissed three people (including her—*third time's the charm*, he says), and things never really kicked off the way they do with her. That's definitely good for her ego, Stevie can't deny it. It's like this primal, probably toxic masculinity (hey, no one's immune), certainly old-fashioned sort of thing, but you feel what you feel, and this? It makes her feel like they've got something special. Something that matters.

There's something about her that *works* for Milo. And everything about him works for Stevie. So, yeah, it's just nice to know they're on the same page.

He kisses her like he really, genuinely likes her, not just the way she makes his body feel. It's hard to know the difference sometimes—she's been around the block maybe not much, but enough to figure that—but Milo makes sure she knows.

It's in the way that he pays attention. He notices when she loosens up or when she tenses, when she speeds up or slows down, and he follows her lead from there. When she's not sure, he pauses to ask her. There's no urgency or impatience to keep going; he wants to make sure that she likes what they're doing right now.

Stevie hopes she's just as thoughtful. She tries to be. She gets caught up in the moment more often, sure, but she knows Milo's tells the same way he knows hers: If his mouth pulls down tight at the corners, she stops what she's doing; if he hums, she keeps going with a little more heat to it; if his hand glides up her waist and clings, she's got free reign to touch him wherever she wants, but she knows not to take it too far and that's why he lets her go for it.

But overall, Milo seems to like it best when he does something *she* likes. Maybe it's another ego thing. The *why* doesn't really matter so long as they're both into it. And, boy, is she *into it* when his mouth curves into a smile against her lips, her skin, her pulse.

If he tastes like sugar, Milo kisses Stevie right back like she's candy.

That is to say... a lot of tongue. Like the last scene of *Clueless* tongue. Which, yeah, it made everyone shriek with equal parts confusion and delight when you first watched it at a junior high sleepover, *but.*

Honestly? The real thing doesn't squick you out as much as you'd think. The real thing is actually kind of awesome?

Even when it's inexpert—maybe especially then. Because then it's all excitement and enthusiasm and it's *fun*. A little gross and messy and *dear God, sticky*, but sex and all its constituents are hardly ever *sexy*, anyway—it's gross and messy, and that doesn't really matter because when you're with someone you like? It's mostly giggling. And tingling. And *nice*.

Also sometimes you accidentally knee somebody in the stomach—all very *Oh my God, I'm sorry!* and *Jesus Christ, woman!*—but you're giggling the whole time then, too.

"Can't have my way with you if you get us *hospitalized*," Milo mumbles, amused, the words pressed into the side of her neck as he goes to town on her.

"Oh, sure, you seem like you're in *immeasurable* pain—" Stevie shrieks when he bites her. He's never done that before, but if she's honest that shriek didn't have any protest in it, *none*, besides the initial surprise.

Milo pauses, breath coming staggered in his chest against her side, in hot bursts over her skin. "Good scream or bad scream?"

Her hand tangles in his curls, the other in his shirt where it's bunched around his belt. "Good."

"Oh. Well"—he licks the spot that's probably on its way to bruising—"you're very loud, then."

"Take it as a compliment."

"Hm." His smile parts wider against her neck when he starts kissing her there again. "Yes, ma'am."

Both of their hands are creeping under each other's shirts, the blunt edges of fingernails scraping hip bones and chasing shivers. Milo's touch is dry, warm, and Stevie knows that her hands are always cold but in this case Milo seems to like it.

His mouth trails to hers, catches her lips deeper, hungrier than usual. Stevie's not complaining; her speed is just the same as Milo's, even when his playlist shuffles to the Vengaboys and they both shake with a combination of want and laughter as "Boom, Boom, Boom, Boom!!" fills the room.

It's not stopping them, not even close. It feels better to laugh in the heat of the moment than to take it too seriously, anyway, urging them on more than it slows them down. Milo's hand in her hair, knuckles kneading the back of her neck, is making those twisty knots in Stevie's stomach go berserk—

"Uh—*whoops*."

It's not the *most* startling realization that they're not alone anymore. But their position is compromising enough, Stevie supposes, that it warrants their reaction to Muppet-yell and spring apart so violently that they topple the chair and roll backwards off it.

That's what she's going to tell herself, anyway—that it was a *reasonable response*, so then at least her bruised elbow will have meaning.

"Jesus." Milo winces as he sits up. "I think I broke my ass."

"Your ass has my apologies." Tatum hoists the recliner right side-up, no harm done, not even a squeak of springs. "Maybe consider this a cautionary tale, like how in horror movies when you get busy, you get"—she mimes stabbing—"*ee-er-ee-er*'d."

"Who knew Milo had it in him?" says—*great*—Whitney. Stevie frowns as she emerges from the hallway, albeit upside-down from Stevie's vantage point still on the floor.

And then Milo blocks her from view, offering Stevie a hand up. He's frowning, too. "Whatever, Whitney."

"Good to see you too."

Milo ignores her and pulls Stevie to her feet. His mouth softens into not quite a smile, but it's closer than it was a second ago. And it widens, too, when he taps a spot on her neck with his thumb and says, so quietly Stevie has to read his lips to catch it, "I think I gave you a hickey."

He's *delighted*. Stevie pushes his face.

"We were just swinging by to see if you felt like going out," Tatum says. "So, yeah, genuinely sorry to interrupt."

"It really didn't cross my mind that there'd be anything *to* interrupt," Whitney adds, would-be innocent if you didn't know her. "Milo's *reeeaaally* not the type and all. I would know, right?" Her laugh is airy, no substance, fake. "So imagine *my* surprise."

"It should come as zero surprise that most people, uh, don't like you," Milo says, would-be friendly if he were saying literally anything else. Hubba hubba, etc. Stevie could start making out with him all over again.

"I think she's okay," Tatum quips, a tad too tightly to be totally funny, like she's trying to break the tension and she's fully aware it's not going to work.

Stevie tries to give her a smile but, yeah, that's about it. It's not Tatum's fault that Whitney is Like This; it's bad timing, that's all.

"I think we'll just see you guys later?" Stevie curls her fingers into the hem of Milo's shirt, gives him a little tug towards her bedroom. Neither of them are much for escape artistry and, even if they were, Whitney's never been one to let things go.

"So much for 'just not being a sexual person,'" she says, air quotes and all. "I never really knew what that meant, anyway."

Milo's smile is gone, jaw set. "Literally just what it sounds like."

"Yeah, because what we walked in on here was so not sexual."

Oh my God, Milo mouths at the ceiling. Then, to Whitney, "You know it's like, really weird that you expect an explanation."

Stevie's not entirely sure what to do here. One second you're macking on your boyfriend, the next his ex shows up to create problems in the household. What is she *supposed* to do?

She exchanges another glance with Tatum, who looks just as lost as that gaping pit in Stevie's gut feels.

"Maybe Nicky should know what she's getting into," Whitney says, like she's making a point that Stevie wants nothing to do with, thanks. "One second a guy says he's into her, the next he won't touch her. I mean, if you need a beard, you can just say so instead of leading someone on."

"*Whoa*," Tatum cuts in. "Whit, come on. Let's just—"

"*You* come on. There's nothing wrong with being gay, he should stop making it everyone else's problem."

Milo snaps—not in a scary way, but more put-off than Stevie's ever seen him, Lars and the guy who got stuck in his pump included. "There is something wrong with you *not listening* to me. It's been three years, dude, are you seriously telling me, in all that time, you haven't thought, like, 'Hey, maybe it's just because Milo's demisexual like he told me he was and I should stop taking it personally'?"

Whitney snaps back at him, with her fingers and everything. "Excuse me if I'm not going to let some guy make me feel bad about myself just because he has *issues*."

Um. Talk about missing the point.

"*Whitney*—"

"*Milo*—"

"No. No way, man." Milo shakes his head, and points at the haughty twitch in Whitney's smirk. "Don't turn this around into something it's not. Don't do that. Think whatever you want about it. You want to think I'm an asshole, fine, but don't turn yourself into some hashtag-girl-power Facebook post when that's *not* what this is about."

"You never even apologized."

"I don't need to apologize for not wanting to have sex!" Milo's voice cracks. The tension in the room does, too, cracks all jagged through the air and nobody knows what else to say to put it back together.

He pushes a hand through his hair, still mussed from Stevie's touch. "Jesus *fuck*, Whitney, what's wrong with you?"

A good question. And one she's not going to entertain.

"Like, for real, Milo? Maybe I just think you're full of shit," Whitney says. Stevie flinches. "And it's time someone calls you out on it. You spend all day talking up sex toys, like you have the experience to talk, I mean..."

A hollow, mean chuckle. "Sorry if I think it's all a little sus."

Milo blinks at her. His own chuckle is more of an incredulous breath. "I want to ask you *what* my job and me not wanting to fuck you have to do with each other, but I also want you to fuck off and leave me alone, so... Yeah." His shoulders drop. "I'm done with this."

He turns to Stevie and asks, just for her to hear, "Hey, will you walk me to my car?"

"Yeah, c'mon." She slips her fingers between his fidgeting ones and—without a look back—leads him outside. She can deal with whatever else Whitney has to say when she gets back; Milo doesn't have to listen to that anymore.

Besides Milo telling her about the less-than-you'd-expect three people he's kissed, this is something they haven't talked about yet—their dating history. Stevie knows Whitney has something to do with Milo's, but she couldn't even tell you if Whitney was one of the three.

She hadn't thought to ask because, after Whitney's initial *been there, done that* comments about Milo, Stevie hadn't given it much thought, period. She'd been too blissed out to worry, or to even really *care*, because it was like Dottie said—Whitney was just trying to psych her out. It didn't truly *matter*.

Guess Stevie was wrong about that.

Super bananas totally *unequivocally* wrong. And she has no idea what to do about it now. She barely knows what to do with her own baggage. She knew it was something she and Milo would have to talk about eventually. You always do, and their Venn diagram of a social circle practically guarantees that Milo and Erik know each other, even just in passing, so it was bound to come up sooner or later.

But Whitney got to them first.

Like hell does Stevie know how to navigate someone else's past, to broach that topic without giving them a piece of yourself to start with.

Stevie hadn't been ready to do that yet. It's still so early, and she and Milo have been having such a good time together, the last thing she'd wanted to do was disrupt that with parents and exes and Other Reasons to Feel Unlovable.

But now, ready or not, it looks like they're going to have to start.

"Milo"—what do you even say?—"I'm so sorry."

"No, don't—you don't have to apologize for her. Or because of her," Milo corrects. They're at the curb, next to his car. He rubs at a spot on the driver's side window. "Trust me, it's—nothing I haven't heard before."

"That doesn't mean you should have to."

He shakes his head. "I'm sorry. I shouldn't have gotten into it with her like that, that was... super not cool of me."

Stevie shrugs. "Whitney really knows how to get to people. She does it to me, too. She even does it to Tatum, and they actually like each other." For some reason.

"I know it's just because she's pissy about... whatever," Milo huffs, scrubs a hand across his mouth. "Because she didn't get what she wanted. She doesn't give a shit about *me*, not as a person. I'm just something that didn't go her way."

The breeze ruffles through his curls, warm and cheery and completely at odds with the weight of this conversation.

"I've seen her around since we ended things," he goes on. "I'm usually better at avoiding her. Now, y'know, she's all bent out of shape because I like someone else—that's you, by the way." His smile is small, a little bit sad, like maybe he thinks that's one-sided now. (Not a chance.) "And she's gotta make it about her. You know how she is."

They're still holding hands. Milo squeezes hers when Stevie gives him her own small, little-bit-sad smile. "You still seem upset."

"Yeah." He sniffs, looks off across the street at nothing. "She was always good at that."

Stevie doesn't know what to say to that. Not that she's known what to say through any and all of this, but she wants to give him *something*.

Before she can, though, Milo takes a breath that sounds like it hurts and then he's off—

"Look, I—can I just tell you this? I don't think I can leave without explaining at least some of it, because the thing with Whitney..." He swallows. Stevie lets him talk. "It's like I said, it was three years ago, I'm way over her. I think I've been over her since the second it ended, I'm just. Not over the way she made me feel, I guess?"

Another sniff. He rubs his nose. "But we met at Loretta's, talked for like a month. It wasn't anything special, but it felt like it was at the time." He looks at his shoes, shuffles his sandal into the grass that's growing too long over the curb. It stains the toe of his sock. "I thought she really liked me."

Stevie nods. She gets it. Whitney's one of those people you just really want to like you—she's hot and confident and she's got really good posture, and maybe those aren't *reasons*, but they're the only things Stevie could ever come up with. There's no one thing she could pinpoint and say *that's it, this is why you want Whitney around.* You just do.

Even Stevie did, at first. Not in a romantic way, but she wanted Whitney to be her friend. She was fun and clever and cutting and cool. But then she started making Tatum cry and doubt herself and be totally unsure of what she wanted. Once that started, Whitney wasn't a person Stevie gave a shit about anymore.

Of course she kept her mouth shut about it. No, she hasn't made it a secret that she doesn't like Whitney, Tatum knows that better than anyone, but she was never about to seriously start giving Tatum *advice.*

Hot tip: your friends don't want your opinion on their love life, not even when they point-blank ask you for it. All you can do is be there for them, so they have someone on their side if things don't work out like you think they won't, but you have to be a better person than to say so.

Stevie desperately wants to be a better person for Milo.

"But then, just..." Milo drums his thumb against Stevie's hand, picks up a beat and goes with it. "One night we were hanging out, and she kind of—right away, she just goes for my belt. She already knew I was demi, and I'd told her I was a take-it-slow kinda guy, and then all of a sudden that wasn't okay with her. So she—"

He sniffs. Scratches his nose again. "I mean, it was like what just happened inside, except worse, I guess, because we didn't have an audience and I didn't expect her to get so mad. I barely even fought back. I just let her say whatever she wanted and I took it. And I—I almost did it, Stevie." He shakes his head. Swallows. His thumb is tapping so fast. "I did, I almost had sex with her just to make her *stop*. I didn't want to feel that way, and for a second I thought if I did what she wanted then I'd stop feeling so fucking bad all the time. But I didn't want to. Like, I didn't want to so *much* that I'd rather feel all messed up and wrong than do something—*normal*."

The words come thick and like they're edged in something sharp, they have to hurt coming out. Stevie doesn't want him to talk about it anymore if he doesn't want to.

"Milo..."

"Shit." He drags a hand over his face, rubs at his watery eyes. "Jesus, Stevie, I'm sorry. This is a lot. I didn't think it would be, I thought I had a handle on all my bullshit, I swear. One second I'm kissing you and it's—it's fucking awesome, seriously, and then we're *here* and I'm just... I'm sorry. I'm a real mess."

"Hey, I—" She tugs at the hand she's still holding, and wraps her free arm around his waist. "I like a little mess, okay? I barely ever even put my laundry away."

He hiccups a laugh and hugs her back. "Yeah. I know."

They stay like that for a minute, quiet and comforting. Milo's warm and he smells like he always does, mint and some generic boy cologne, nothing special—she couldn't tell you if it was *bergamot* or *cinnamon* or *woodsmoke* or any of those romantic kind of words—but it's become Stevie's favorite smell in the world.

He presses a kiss to the side of her face, between her temple and where her cheekbone starts, and pulls back just enough to look at her.

"I know there's a lot we need to talk about, especially after this whole shitshow. I just—can you give me a couple of days?" He strokes a thumb across her cheek and keeps it there. "I need to just... calm down, I guess. I can't explain anything to you the way I want when I'm all messed up like this."

Anxiety clogs her throat, sticky and viscous. She doesn't want to give him a couple of days. Stevie knows it's wrong, and selfish, and just a *phenomenally* asshole move—especially after what he's just told her, *God*, what is *wrong* with her?—but she doesn't want to give him the opportunity to decide that he doesn't want to do this with her, after all.

But it's not about her.

So she nods, unsticks her throat the best she can, and she tells him, "Of course. Hey, I'm—I'm here whenever you want to talk about it."

He's frowning slightly, but looking at her so *earnestly*, too. "This isn't me ghosting you. Okay?"

Is she smiling? She's trying to, to reassure him, but it can't be coming across right. "Okay."

"I'll text you tonight," Milo promises. "Not about... all this. But. Just to talk to you."

"If you need time to think things over, you don't have to do that. Really."

"I want to. *Really.*" His smile is more reassuring than hers was, probably. "To be, uh, super not chill at all about it, I can't go a day without talking to you. That's no way to live, baby face."

It's a joke, or he tries to make it one, but, yeah. She knows the feeling.

"Stevie." Milo slips his hand down to cradle her jaw, make her look at him. He's not teasing anymore, not even trying to. "I promise I'm not going anywhere."

When she tries to smile this time, she thinks she might actually pull it off. "Okay."

And when Milo kisses her, she kisses him back—a good one, all the way down to her toes, one that will last. Not to be all teen angst about it, because she heard what he said and she believes him, but she's still scared and she can't help it.

This isn't me ghosting you. I promise I'm not going anywhere.

But what if he changes his mind?

ALEXA, PLAY "LET'S TALK ABOUT SEX" BY SALT-N-PEPA

S ometimes—and *understandably*, thank you—Milo thinks about quitting his job cold-turkey and just, walking into the woods, never to be seen again.

Not that he's got the survival skills to cut it in the woods, and more's the pity—though, it is suburban Indiana, *the woods* is really just a sparse backyard behind a Dairy Queen, maybe an Arby's, either way civilization's like a ten-minute walk from wherever you are—but *the point is*... Sometimes Milo never wants to talk to another human being ever again.

Those *sometimes* are almost entirely thanks to Bryce.

He's twenty-something-or-other, good-looking in that bland sort of way where you couldn't pick him out of a lineup—he is very much Just Some Fuckin' Guy—and he doesn't ask questions when he comes in, no, he's only here to gripe.

He's Milo's responsibility. He won't talk to Penn, which is just as well because Penn won't talk to him, either, even today, when Milo's in *a mood* and they're sharing shift since Saturday afternoons get some decent traffic.

But Bryce won't talk to Penn because "Well I know how you *females* get about this sort of thing," and Penn said "I literally *work here*, dude," and Bryce just *hmph*'d and smirked and rolled his eyes. For surely obvious reasons, Penn didn't bother to correct him on the subject of gender identity.

Anyway. It was a whole thing. Milo doesn't want to talk to him, either.

Terminally insecure and real fucking annoying about it, Bryce's latest problem is that he doesn't understand what his girlfriend needs a vibrator for.

"Man—" Milo heaves a deep, long-suffering (and *oh*, how he is *suffering* right now) sigh, slumped over the counter. How does he always end up here? (Rhetorical question.) "Bryce. My dude. You're not *competing with* her vibrator. What you're thinking here, that's fucking... *foolishness*, man."

"I just don't get how it works," Bryce complains, like he's not a fully adult man with internet access.

"Double-A batteries, usually," Penn quips, but flatly so, from where they're restocking bedroom dice on the game wall. Bryce ignores them.

"Women, y'know, they're just gonna compare you to it. It messes with the whole relationship. I don't think she should have it."

Milo really. Cannot listen to this anymore.

Because, *y'know*, it's guys like Bryce who have no problem bagging whoever they've got their eye on. Guys like Bryce who have some inherent skill or charisma or *something* that distracts from all their whining. Bryce and Erik and Lars and a dozen other guys who are in and out of the store, and yet never seem to goddamn *learn* anything.

Milo can't even kiss a girl without blowing it up.

And, fine, so he knows that kissing Stevie isn't what messed things up. He knows, even, that *he* didn't mess things up so much as he... Okay, he doesn't know what he did, exactly. It's more that *he is who he is*, and—thank you, Whitney—who he is isn't conducive to boyfriend material.

But of course he still *wants* to be Stevie's boyfriend. It's been two days since he asked her for some time and space to get his shit together, and for the most part Milo's managed to do that. He's not pissed off about Whitney anymore—not more than usual—but he's not digging this hopeless resignation thing he's doing now any better, where he can't imagine why Stevie would want to bother with him anymore.

He needs to talk to her.

He just needs to get through today first.

So, naturally, today has been, in a word, *impossible*. Because *today*, Bryce is back to bitch and moan about how his girlfriend can find her own clit (*oh, unknowable universe, how could you do this to Bryce*), meanwhile Milo's got his own self-inflicted punctured ego—and six boxes of inventory—to get through. So *excuuuuuuse* the fuck outta him if he's at his wit's end.

Milo covers his face with his hands and groans at Bryce, who is somehow *still talking*.

"Dude. *Dude*." Milo cuts him off with another deep sigh. Lucky thing they've got enough of a rapport that Bryce doesn't complain when Milo talks shit, so *talk shit* he does, and *enthusiastically* (exasperatedly, really, but he doesn't hold back).

"If you start picking fights with your girlfriend about her vibrator, you're not gonna *have* a girlfriend anymore, because she's gonna think you suck, and not in the way she wants."

"See, it does cause a problem."

"Yeah, if the problem is that you're a *man-child*."

Bryce's scowl is more like a pout, such is the way of properly chastised straight men. "You're such a prick sometimes."

"I'm *helping you*, dickweed. You're jealous of a *bullet*," Milo says like it's embarrassing. *Which it is.* "Quit whining and use it on her the next time she agrees to have sex with you for some reason."

Regardless of rapport and despite the leeway that comes with the job, Milo doesn't usually talk to people like this. *Usually* he retains some sense of decorum. He's here to help, he *wants* to help, but Bryce doesn't want help, which makes Milo's mood all the worse for wear.

He's on edge, he's been pissed off at himself for days and he doesn't know how to fix it, and if he's gonna take it out on some poor unsuspecting passersby, it might as well be Bryce. *To reiterate*, the dude makes Milo want to walk into the woods, never to be seen again, but he's also a pretty guilt-free outlet for your suppressed issues.

"Well, why *would* she want to have sex with me again?" Bryce says, with the kind of passive aggression reserved for *Degrassi* bullies before they get their redemption arc. "If she's got her precious *vibrator*."

God. God!

Milo needs to, like, *find his center*, because he really can't live off his part-time gig at the auto shop. He's worked in customer service long enough to be used to this, this is how it goes—and he's *so close* to his allotted vacation time; all he has to do is simply not commit murder today.

That's showbiz, baby.

"Bryce." Milo pinches the bridge of his nose to stave off the surely imminent stress bleeding. "Bryson. Brycetopher. Listen.

Come on. You're taking this way too personally. Her vibe is your *friend*. You want her to come, don't you?"

"I can do it myself."

Mmmmm, Milo's not so sure about that, but—"Missing the point, Brycearoni."

There's no arguing with this guy. He only comes here to get Milo to tell him what he wants to hear, and Milo never does. Not out of spite—although that would be *fair*—but because Bryce is *never right*. Not once, not even a little bit, no matter how much he insists. The man is *powerfully* self-deluded.

"He's a fascinating social experiment, isn't he?" Penn says, after Bryce calls it, buys a novelty pack of dirty-words gum, and leaves.

Milo tosses the cash drawer back into place with a satisfying *ching* and *click*. "You say that about everyone who comes in here."

"And *you* say that like we didn't take this job for the same reason and that's it."

Milo snorts, pretends to review his inventory sheet. "I'm just trying to pay my rent and, like, *eat* at the same time."

"Uh-huh." Gotta love the derision. "Wanna talk about it?"

He doesn't bother deflecting; he knows what Penn means. Milo had texted the group chat, because he'd wanted them to know but he didn't want to talk about it, that he'd had a run-in with Whitney and he's worried he's messing things up with Stevie and he'd let them know if he totally loses it. Until then—

"Nope," Milo says. He gives up on inventory, too distracted to double-check counts of lube samples, and starts taking the display vibrators down from wall mounts to clean them.

Not that anyone's *using* them, mind, but they collect dust and fingerprints like a crime scene.

It follows, of course, naturally, *cosmically*, that as *ardently* as Milo doesn't want to talk about something, a mass conspiracy arises to make him: Enter Tatum in a flurry of paisley sundress and go-go boots, swinging into the store like she owns it, and making a beeline for Milo like she's about to ruin his life.

Why are all of his friends like this?

(*This*, he thinks, has got to be the encapsulation of the queer experience. Artemis was right—staying out of your friends' business really is a straight people thing.)

She knocks her knuckles against the counter. Milo sprays her hands with the store-issued bottle of toy cleaner.

"Ask me what I've been up to this week."

Milo sets aside a remote-controlled egg and intones dully, barely an inflection at the end, "What've you been up to this week, Tatum."

"I'm glad you asked." She gives the counter a drumroll. "First, I dumped Whitney."

Milo debates between *About time* and *How long's it gonna last this time?* before he decides to not be a total dick about it.

"You didn't have to do that. *Should*," Milo allows, "but didn't have to. Not on my account."

"Look, I won't pretend I know everything that happened with you guys. I don't need to," Tatum says. "She said some fucked-up stuff to you, and even if you were okay about it, I'm not. It made Stevie cry."

A knot twists in Milo's throat. "She cried?"

"Don't make that face. *You* didn't make her cry. She's just..." Tatum deliberates. "Frustrated."

That doesn't make him feel better. He still should have been there.

He'd known Stevie was upset, he could see it all over her face; it's part of why he tried so hard to convince her that he wasn't ditching her, and that ditching her is the absolute, definitely, definitively, *last thing* he wants.

It's just that there's a lot to say, to explain, before they can keep going, and Milo doesn't really know how to do that anymore. Because every other time he's tried, well... Whitney had been the worst of it, but everyone before her hadn't been much better.

Tatum frowns at his silence. "You're not trying to break up with her, are you?"

Penn joins the conversation with a laugh—*fine* time for the store to have a lull. "More like he's trying to figure out a way to propose. Get that pussy on lock, you know how it is."

"*Jesus*, Penn—" Milo curses. He fumbles one of the more temperamental models, and the thing starts jackhammering its way across the counter to the beat of Milo's own nervous heart.

Tatum catches the runaway rabbit, clicks it off, and whacks him in the ribs with it. Not hard enough to hurt, just to keep his attention. Then she starts *gesturing* at him with it.

(There's a Billy Idol song on the speakers now, too, and Milo doesn't know why that makes everything more *ridiculous*, but—well. You try getting lectured by one of your friends while they gesticulate with a garishly purple vibrator and "Dancing with Myself" soundtracks your pent-up anxiety, *then* you can tell Milo his life isn't some cosmically orchestrated *Truman Show* rip-off.)

"You can't tell a girl you'll *talk about it later*," Tatum berates him. "Have you never watched any popular media in the history of all time? That's code for 'We're probably going to break up.' Or 'I want to become the Ultimate Fighting Champion.'"

Penn taps their temple to shake the reference loose. "*Friends*, right?"

"Got it in one. And let's face it, Milo, you're no Jon Favreau. Look at you." Tatum brandishes the vibrator some more. "You'd be *eaten alive*."

"Yeah, so was Jon Favreau," Milo reminds her. He levels the bulbous end of a wand right back at her, and just as accusingly. "You're losing your own point here."

"Right, well, my point is"—Tatum whacks the wand out of her face—"the heteros got something right, and it's that you can't say leading, cryptic shit like that and then disappear. *Poof.*"

"I didn't *poof*." Milo snatches the vibrator out of her hand and sets it aside, out of reach. "I'm still texting her, just like normal."

But even as he says it, Milo wants to punch himself in the face. No way could any slew of memes and *good mornings* and heart emojis relieve his guilt. He's doing what he promised, but there's plenty more he needs to do.

"It's *not* 'just like normal,'" Tatum argues, calling him on it the way Milo should have been doing to himself, "because she knows something's wrong. And she knows it's not her fault, and it's not yours, either, but it's still like, this big deal thing you guys have to talk about. I'm not saying you have to talk about it before you're ready, just, cut me some slack here, Milo. I just dumped the hottest chick I've ever been with and my best friend's been listening to her sad girl playlist for two days."

Tatum scowls. She's much better at it than Bryce. "How many times do you think I can hear 'I Can't Make You Love Me' before I'm gonna wanna kick your ass?"

"What's your problem with Bonnie Raitt?"

"*Nothing*, I'm not a lunatic, but it's a pretty vast overreaction, don't you think?" Tatum says. "Because Stevie doesn't think so, and it's a mondo bummer to see your friend all broken-hearted when she doesn't need to be. Because her feelings are already hurt but also she's being stupid."

Right. Yeah. That's—not what he meant to do. So of course that's exactly what happened. Look, Milo's just been trying not to fuck this up, okay? He's seen enough nonsensical angsty romantic dramas that are drama for like, no other reason except *aesthetic* or whatever—why don't these people just *talk* to each other, you know? It doesn't make a good movie, he guesses, but at least it wouldn't be so fucking stupid—to know better.

So, yeah, Tatum's right—whether he's got his ducks in a row or not (and who ever does? There's ducks all over the fuckin' place), he needs to talk to Stevie. *Really* talk to her, about all the shit he's been too scared to tell her in case it changes her mind about him.

She likes him. He *knows* that. Why can't he believe in it?

Milo pulls out his phone and, as he texts Stevie to come by after his shift, please, he says to their friends (who are in the middle of a celebratory two-person wave), "For future reference, I think I prefer it when Dottie's the one telling me I'm being a dumbass."

"She has a *PhD*," Penn says. "Who else among us has that kind of stamina?"

"Right." Tatum snaps her fingers, points. "We can't all have Dottie's credentials."

"Yeah," Milo agrees, only half-involved in this discussion he started since Stevie texted back to say she'd be there. (It's very *thank God* but also *oh, no*, ya dig?) "But she wouldn't try concussing me with a vibrator, either."

"Well, then, how would you ever *learn*?"

Milo's sure there has to be a logical and mature answer to that question. He doesn't know it, so he sprays Tatum in the face with the toy cleaner instead.

***

At the far end of the strip mall, behind the taco place, there's a courtyard with plastic picnic tables where Milo goes to wait for Stevie. It smells like fried tortillas and cigarette smoke, maybe a dash of cheap pot. It's grounding, somehow.

He sits on one of the tabletops, traces the Sharpie graffiti next to him just to give his twitchy fingers something to do. He'd rather not occupy himself with his thoughts—God, no—and anyway there's not much going on upstairs except for the gentle thrum of his anxiety.

And when Stevie turns the corner into the courtyard, walking toward him with two takeout sodas in hand—BAM!—no gentle thrum about it, his heart goes off like a malfunctioning bottle rocket.

Her hair's up in a fluffy bun, aviators on, a loose tank top tucked into denim joggers, a flannel tied around her waist, her bumblebee Crocs. The latest nose ring is a ladybug to match her tattoo.

She always looks so fucking *cute*, and hasn't that been the problem from the start? A problem that shouldn't be a problem, and yet here he is, absolutely mired in trouble.

"Hi." Her smile is small, nervous, and Milo wants to kiss it into its big, real shape. Now's not the time, but he resolves to get there before the day is through.

He knocks his foot against the side of her knee. "Hi."

She hands him one of the comically large sodas, the ones you get from Panda Express when you order a large and they mishear it as "Fuck me up with a bucket of Fanta."

After a grateful sip, he talks around his straw. "You know it's half-off smoothies today?"

"I figured this would be more of a, um." Stevie pops her lips thoughtfully. "Full-fat cola beverage conversation?"

Oh, God, he likes her so much. "You made the right choice."

Stevie twirls a hand, takes a bow.

"Not to ruin your moment," Milo says through his grin, because he knows they've got a lot to talk about, but sue him if she makes him smile, okay. "But, uh. I talked to Tatum."

"I—right." Stevie grimaces. "She told me she talked to you, then gave me her keys and was like, *now it's your turn.* Which. Yeah. But, um." She flicks at the condensation sweating down her cup. "What did she say?"

"Bonnie Raitt was mentioned."

Her cheeks go blotchy pink like a sunburn. "Oh."

"She's worried about you," Milo tells her, and it's with no small measure of guilt. *I am, too.*

"I'm fine. Really." Stevie sighs, steps onto the bench and sits next to him on the tabletop. "I'm sorry, Milo, you don't need to be worried about me, this isn't about me. I was just... worried."

Another sigh, and she mumbles into a pull from her drink, "Word of the day, I guess."

"I promise you don't need to be." He wishes he had some way to prove it that was more than just saying it. "But I, uh, I get it. I'm worried, too."

The frown that crosses her mouth is slight, confused.

"What about?" Stevie angles her body towards him, one leg tucked underneath her the same way she sits in his car. The move makes Milo's chest go tight and warm. *Fluttery.*

She does this to him all the time, and the way she smiles at him sometimes? He thinks he does it to her, too. It's not just the feeling, either, it's that it happens with *Stevie.* He doesn't want to lose her.

That's what he's worried about.

"Ah." He lifts his gaze to the almost-overcast sky. "Where to start..."

"Is this about Whitney?"

"Yes and no?" Milo really doesn't want to rehash what he's already told Stevie—it was more than he'd ever told anyone else, even his friends—but that's as good a place to start as any.

Go big or go home, right? And he's not ready to leave.

"It's more like, she's a symptom of the problem," he explains, or tries to, "and *I'm* the problem. Because I'm demi, so I don't want to have sex just to have it, so it's my fault if I make someone feel bad or insecure or unlovable. No matter how honest I am with them, it doesn't matter, because the way I feel isn't as important as their self-esteem."

"That's not true."

"Logically, yeah, I know that. Emotionally? Not so much. It's like—"

He chews on the edge of his thumbnail, unsure of how to put this. What he lands on isn't the best way to put things, but it's a jumping-off point he can work with.

"Do you remember, when you were telling me about disco and how, like, the sexual liberation of it all made it for everyone?" When Stevie nods, Milo goes on. "I get that, but at the same time I don't *get that*. I don't *feel* that. Like I know it's a good thing, and I'm not trying to detract from that, but I also just..."

He frowns at his straw, bends it back and forth. "I know I'm reading too much into it, probably? But it just, it speaks to this whole bigger, *other* issue for me, because I feel so disconnected from that kind of thing. Like it's not for me, even though I'm supposed to be a part of this community. I just, I don't feel like I *fit*."

Yeah, that about does it.

"Which is like, a super self-involved take," Milo admits. "I probably sound like an asshole, but... Well, whatever, I'm already a solid six, six and a half, I can't have a perfect moral code, too."

"First of all, you're a ten. You *are*," Stevie insists when he snorts. "And I get what you mean. I do. We all want to think we're good enough people that we're just, completely incandescently happy for other people when things work out for them. But when we're not in the same place?"

She shrugs. She's bending her straw, too. "Yeah, I think it's natural to feel resentment or hurt or just, *something* unpleasant. It doesn't make you an asshole."

Maybe not. Like he said, it's not really about the disco thing, anyway; his thoughts just snowballed from there.

Milo pops the bubbles on the lid of his cup. *Coke—Diet Coke—Root Beer—Other*. When he was a kid, before he could read, he didn't realize those were labels. He thought it was some kind of game that nobody knew the rules for. He'd pop them all, pause for dramatic effect, and say, "I don't get it."

There's a metaphor here somewhere. Or maybe it's even more on-the-nose than that. It makes sense to him, though; ever since he figured out he was demisexual, it's always made sense. Milo understands himself, the definition is enough for him: He doesn't experience sexual feelings unless there's an emotional connection first. That's it. It should be easy, right?

But the way he *feels*? There's no way to explain that. None that he's found, anyway.

He doesn't know how else to say it: he just wants to *fit*. And even in a community where people go to find that place, he still hasn't.

"I just, I can understand myself and be proud of myself all I want, but there's something that feels... *wrong* with me. I feel like I'm not allowed to be in this space," he continues, determined to make sure that Stevie *gets it*. He wants her to get it, so badly. "You heard what Whitney said, that I shouldn't be ashamed if I was gay. But I'm not gay, so it's like—I'm not *queer enough*, whatever that even means, but I'm sure as shit not straight, so where does that leave me?"

Almost in tears, is where it leaves him. If he were to be one hundred and ten percent honest and cut-me-open-bleeding vulnerable about it, that's where he is.

Milo swipes at his eyes. "Sometimes it's like coming out didn't even make a difference, you know? Because no matter what I say, nobody gets how I feel."

He has his friends, and it's not like they're assholes—alright, so the virginity jokes get a little old, fine—and Dottie's got her own asexual experience, she can relate. But outside that bubble? He's never been able to make something work.

It's a whole other thing to meet someone who won't hold it against you. It's something else to meet someone you want to be with, who wants to be with you, too, who doesn't change their mind at a complete one-eighty because they take your sexuality personally.

Because that's what it is—they make it about *them*, about Milo making them feel unwanted. Like he's the problem factor here, like sex is the only way to show someone you want them.

He's just so tired of understanding where everyone else is coming from, when no one else will try for him.

He's tired of *everything* being about sex. Because everything is, everything seems to boil down to that, and most people don't seem to mind or even notice because it doesn't affect the core of who they are. But Milo feels it everywhere—this pressure. He's never even had sex and he's already sick of it.

But he wants this thing with Stevie, too, and it's like he can't reconcile both parts of himself into something that makes sense to him. Because he's so sick of all the bullshit expectations, all the *pressure*, but he wants to give in to these feelings for Stevie, and how can both those things be true? It's like he's got imposter syndrome about *being a human person*.

Penn told him that he's not a dictionary definition, that he doesn't owe anyone *more* when they don't accept what he gives them. Artemis told him to have a little faith, that things aren't always such a colossal fuck-up and he never deserved for them to be. Dottie's always telling him that *normal* isn't a real thing, but the way you feel is, so why bother aiming for something that's not achievable when you can take care of what you've got?

And Stevie told him she likes him just the way he is.

Maybe he should start believing the people who care about him, more than the people who never cared enough to listen.

"Milo?" Stevie bumps her knuckles against his hip. "Listen, I—I think you know where I'm at with us. But I want you to be there, too. It's okay if you're not. If we need to do this differently, or if—if you don't want to do this at all—"

"That's not it." Milo shakes his head, turns to face her. He curls a hand around her knee. "Not even close. I'm just—Jesus, Stevie, I'm scared I'm not gonna do it *right.*"

It's nuts, because he spends so much time *knowing* that so many people do it wrong—he hears it all the time at the store, he sees it happen with his friends, he knows how people mess it up. He wants to think that he's seen enough to know better.

But what's the point of knowing better, if he's too scared to try?

He didn't think he was scared, not really, not *debilitatingly.* He thought he was doing okay, that he was getting past all the bullshit, because things were going so well with Stevie and he was *happy.* But then... Well, it's like he told her the other day: He's way over Whitney, over all his scant number of exes and almosts; but he's not over all the bad ways they made him feel.

He doesn't know if he'll ever get over it. But if he can't move on *from* it, he can still try to move on *with* it.

And he wants to move on with Stevie.

"I'd kind of... resigned myself, I guess?" he tells her now. "To the fact that maybe this just wouldn't happen for me. And that's—that's crazy, I get it, because I'm only thirty, but—"

Milo sighs. He keeps his gaze steady on Stevie's knee, where he's tracing patterns around a teensy rip in the seam of her joggers.

"You just, you try enough times and it doesn't work out, and it's always in this way that feels like it's *your fault*, you know? Because it wasn't just Whitney, it was *everyone*. I was always the one who didn't want to hook up. I didn't want to take things physical. So then I missed my chance on something."

Stevie dips her head to catch his eye. He glances away, embarrassed, when she says, "It sounds more like they missed their chance on you."

That funny thrum reverberates around his heart. "Yeah, well. I guess sex is a better deal than I am."

"I don't think so."

Now his eyes lock on hers. "You sure? Because I—I really don't know when I'm gonna be ready for that."

He wants to tell her *Because I really like you* and *I want you so much it makes me fucking panic*, but how can he tell her all that in the same breath as *I'm not ready for sex*? Won't that just confuse her more?

Hell, it confuses *him*, and they're his feelings.

"I really like you, Milo," Stevie tells him. And he knew that, he did, but he'll never want her to stop saying it. "And that doesn't just happen, you know? Because you're right—when you take sex off the table, a lot of people, they just... write you off. And I *like* sex, but when that's all it is..."

She shakes her head. "I don't know. It doesn't make me feel good, either, not when they want to hook up because I'm, like, a 'sure thing.' *Seriously*," she clarifies when Milo wrinkles his nose in distaste. "The way people talk about bisexuality sometimes, it's like I'm not even a person. I'm a—sex doll. Like that's all I'm for. I don't even get to want anything else."

"So what is it?" Milo prompts her when she pauses, lingering over her words. "That you want?"

"You. And that's not a come-on," Stevie adds quickly. "I mean, I don't expect you to—to striptease for me, or something—"

"That's. An oddly specific scenario."

"*Specific.* I didn't even name a song!"

"Bet you've got one, though."

"*Everyone's* got a striptease song. And it's *always* 'Pour Some Sugar On Me.'"

"Who are you, every dad in the Midwest? This is blatant Ginuwine erasure. 'Pony' has a way better beat for a—a—" Milo snaps his fingers, searching for the right word.

"Dance of the seven veils?"

He stops snapping to point at her, accusatory. "*Catholic.*"

She shrugs, smiles. "It's a, uh. *Bizarro* story."

"There's at least half a dozen SVU episodes probably inspired by it."

"Only half a dozen?"

"Well, yeah, sometimes they gotta mix it up." Milo runs his hand up her thigh, fingers tapping. "Put a tiger in someone's apartment, you know how it goes."

Stevie laughs. "I like you, Milo."

"Oh, right. That's what we were talking about. I, um. I like you too, for the record." Loves her, really, but one thing at a time. "Which is... It's not something I say a lot? Because it's usually like, 'Then why won't you have sex with me?', which I'm pretty sure is something they warned us about in junior high sex ed, actually."

"Probably the only accurate thing they taught us. I sure think it was my major takeaway," Stevie adds. She tugs on his sleeve, seriousness settling into the corners of her mouth where that laugh had just been. "Because, yeah, we never have to have sex, not if it's something you don't want. It doesn't change the way I feel about you, Milo. It doesn't make this less important."

Her breath trembles for a second before she talks her way through it. "I really want you to know that, okay? Being with someone isn't about sex. It's about that someone, you know? And you—you're really my someone. Meeting you and getting to know you and... everything... None of it's been about me wanting a relationship. It's about how much I want to be with you."

She catches his hand in hers. "I want to do this with you, whatever this looks like for us."

"Jesus." Milo tries to swallow his heart in his throat, put it back where it belongs. "Sweep me off my feet in thirty seconds or less."

Stevie presses her lips together, nervous, bashful. She stares at their hands while Milo laces their fingers together. "I feel like maybe you could use a little wooing for once."

"Well, fuck me, you're really good at it!"

"It's all the Bonnie Raitt."

"And Tatum wants to kick my ass for that? Shoot." Milo's whistle cuts straight through Stevie's giggle. "Fuck it, you keep talking to me like that, I'll let her hit me with her car."

"So I did okay, then?"

"Baby face." Milo plants a kiss on her palm before he lets her go, so he can move both hands to Stevie's cheeks, freckled and pink and twitching with the promise of her smile. "Everything you do is my favorite thing in the world."

"Oh, good." And *there it is*, that's what he's talking about: her smile—big and real, deeply dimpled, and it coats all of Milo's worries in candy hearts. "You're my favorite, too."

***

Milo Lamoree is In A Relationship with Stevie Hart
42 likes • 17 comments

Artemis Bello: You've got no footprint on social media for the better part of your adult life, and now you show up to tell us something we already know?
(2 likes)

Milo Lamoree: yah
(2 likes)

Stevie Hart: it's really just for documentation purposes, we both get very confused
(3 likes)

Milo Lamoree: it's true, we do
(Stevie Hart likes this)

Dottie Carmichael: We already know that, too.
(5 likes)

Tatum O'Leary: OUCH. And that's from a -therapist-!
(Dottie Carmichael likes this)

Milo Lamoree: @Dottie, ur fired again

Dottie Carmichael: BFFLs <3
(6 *likes*)

June Lamoree: Dear Milo— Your father and I are so excited
to meet your new girlfriend! But please be nicer to your friends,
also. Love, Mom
(14 *likes*)

Penn Valerie: L M A O

Artemis Bello: @June we're obsessed with you
(7 *likes*)

June Lamoree: Thank you, Artemis :) And hello, Stevie!
(2 *likes*)

Milo Lamoree: @June mom you have to tag her

June Lamoree: Oh! You know I don't know what that means.
Why don't you just tell her for me?

Milo Lamoree: ......stevie says hi
(4 *likes*)

June Lamoree: :D Love you all!
(11 *likes*)

YOU MUST BE THIS TALL TO RIDE THE EMOTIONAL ROLLERCOASTER

When Milo walks into the duplex (the door left unlocked since he texted on his way over), it's to find Stevie laying on the floor, aggravated groaning barely decipherable over Smokey Robinson & The Miracles on the Bluetooth.

"The Tracks of My Tears," to be precise. Milo frowns. Does she think he broke up with her? Surely not—they just had this conversation a couple of weeks ago. This relationship's got legs, baby, and they've been taking things at a steady jog.

(Maybe more of a leisurely walk. Milo's not sure; he really doesn't do enough cardio for this metaphor to fly.)

Or! This has something to do with why Stevie asked if he would please pick her up some pads and a bottle of vodka. Yeah. It's probably that.

He'd brought Taco Bell, too, as a precautionary measure, because if nothing else he knew Stevie was in an Emotional State, and usually that calls for a bacon club Chalupa or several.

He pokes his head into her eye line, holding up the goods. "Your rations, ma'am."

"*Thank you.*" Stevie sniffles, her eyes are red, the whole thing.

"Why are you crying?!" He shakes the vodka bottle. "I got the pink kind!"

"It's not that." She turns the volume down on the music, but she doesn't say anything else like Milo thought she would, just sighs so heavily that it's basically another groan. He prods her with his foot.

"Tell me your feelings."

"Ugh."

"You have to."

Because, you see, it turns out that being honest about your thoughts, feelings, insecurities, and your own personal human condition in general does wonders for the open lines of communication in your relationship. *Who knew?*

None of the teen soaps Milo grew up watching religiously, that's for sure. But that's what he gets for putting any faith in *One Tree Hill* whatsoever, so, y'know. Live and learn.

If he thought things with Stevie were on the right track before—*before* when he was pretending to have a deep and meaningful understanding of his emotions, only to be proven *thoroughly incorrect* at the first sign of trouble (but! C'est la vie!)—now that he's taken responsibility for his bad feelings? He gets to coast on the good ones, too.

(You know that song from *Flashdance*? It's like that.)

(...Milo had to ask Stevie, just to double-check, but it's "What A Feeling." Not "Maniac." That one's irrelevant. Still a banger, though.)

Stevie *had* seemed just as happy as him. They're back to all the giggles and flirting and super-obnoxious-to-other-people behavior, like they'd been at the start, only now it's underscored with this very finite understanding of one another. Milo doesn't know how else to explain it but to call it *stable*. He's relaxed, comfortable, and Stevie has been, too. But—you don't lay on the floor groaning to break-up music when things are going *well*.

Right?

Or is this a menstruation thing? Milo likes to think he's all compassionate and understanding, but he doesn't know the *rituals*.

When he points this out, Stevie just laughs in his face. She's still on the floor and everything, so it's not totally *in his face*, actually, but Milo feels pretty rigorously chastised all the same. He hands over the vodka as penance.

She sits up to twist the cap and comfortably take a pull. "My mom called me today."

That's all she gives him. Not surprising; Stevie's more of a closed book—not in an *aloof* way, but a John-Mulaney-voice "I'll keep all my emotions right here, and then one day I'll die" way.

So. Looks like Milo's gonna have to wring the feelings out of her like a sponge.

"And we... hate your mother?"

"Not exactly?" Stevie nestles the bottle in the cradle of her thighs, drums her palms against the insides of them the way she does when she's wound-up. "We're more... stressed out about my mother. Or, I am. You probably don't have anything to worry about."

"*Probably?*"

"I don't know yet, she doesn't know about you."

"Stevie. Please," Milo says, as deadpan as he can (he's been getting better at it, hanging out with her so much). "All this affection. You're suffocating me."

"You just—will you sit down, please, you're already like a foot taller than me."

Milo drops the pharmacy and Taco Bell bags onto the coffee table, and joins her on the floor like the very sophisticated and emotionally stable adults that they are. He spreads his arms, twirls his hands, invites her to continue.

"It's not actually anything to do with you, like, *in particular,*" Stevie explains. "It was just a normal phone call, small talk or whatever. I just, I don't talk to them about my love life. My stepdad is, like, a *guy's guy,* you know? And my mom... I don't know." Another swig from the bottle. "I've just never been like that with my mom."

Hm. Maybe that really is all there is to it. That defeated slump of her shoulders says otherwise, but Milo's not going to press the issue if she's not willing to talk about it on her own yet. Where would he even start? He's always had an easy-peasy relationship with his parents, so trying to commiserate with anybody who doesn't would just make him really fucking annoying, probably.

Besides, Stevie gave him space when he needed it, when he wasn't ready to talk about what he needed to talk about, and she was there when he sorted himself out; he can do the same for her.

"Well, as you have been made *well* aware, my mom is very excited about you. You can borrow her," Milo offers. He snags the vodka and takes his own swig. "If she and Dad ever come back from their cruise, which, honestly? We might never see them again."

"Who could blame them?" Stevie makes grabby hands at the Taco Bell bag, which Milo dutifully passes to her. She unwraps the first of four Chalupas (listen, Milo's like, in love with her, okay, it's always four Chalupas *at least*) and takes what can only be described as an *alarming* bite. She must be in an even more Emotional State than Milo thought.

"What do you want to do tonight?"

Okie dokie, definitely done with the parentals conversation, then.

So much for wringing Stevie's feelings out of her like a sponge, but Milo gives in easily. It's like he said—she needs the space, he'll give it to her.

"Everyone's going to Loretta's if you're up for it? Otherwise we can just hang out here, SVU it up."

Those seem like safe suggestions. Normal, breezy. They've spent more time marinating in Milo's feelings than Stevie's, that's for sure, so he's not positive how to tread here, but *business as usual* feels like the way to go. What other options does he have?

(Give him a break. There must be a learning curve to being a boyfriend, right?)

He shrugs into a bite of one of his crunchy tacos, sucks at the lettuce that gets stuck on his lip. Total class act. "Whatever you feel like doing, I'm easy."

"Let's go out," she says, somewhat surprising him. It must show on his face—so much for *breezy*—because Stevie's mouth twitches like it does when she's uncomfortable.

"I really just, I don't want to sit here all night stewing about my mommy issues." She promptly moves on before Milo can consider coaxing the feelings out of her, after all. "Plus my cramps don't feel so bad when I'm out doing something. If we stay here I'll just keep groaning, you won't even be able to enjoy Ice-T's one-liners."

"And then it's hardly even SVU," Milo agrees. He takes another bite, another second to mull over his limited options.

But in the end, did he honestly think he was going to do anything except whatever she wants?

"Alright, we'll go." Another bite. Tortilla crumbles down his shirt. "If it gets too crowded we can just go make out in my car."

Stevie brushes crumbs off his collar. "Smooth."

Milo clicks his tongue, winks at her, all with a full mouth. "Like butta, baby."

***

"...I'm just saying! I don't get the people who try to prank call a sex store. We're not Target, so if you call asking for a ten-inch dildo, yeah, *we have it*. What's the joke?"

"Oh my God." Artemis titters into his amaretto sour. "I love your job. Mostly because it's not mine."

"That's very helpful, thanks."

They're at a high-top at the back wall of Loretta's, under one of those big felt posters of dogs playing poker, except these dogs are all dolled up as famous drag queens and kings. Milo has *no earthly idea* where they got it, but rumor has it that it was a gift from God.

It's Friday—*Casual Friday*, to be exact, so everyone's in lounge clothes or straight-up PJs—and, as such, the place is pretty hoppin', but Stevie seems okay. Tatum's working and the rest of them—Milo (tank top, basketball shorts), Artemis (silk pants and a for real *smoking jacket*, because he's better than everyone else), Dottie (one of her husband's college T-shirts, bike shorts), and Penn (mismatched flannel shirt and shorts)—are here to hang out.

Stevie (Oscar the Grouch cami, cuffed sweatpants) is sitting at the end of the table, with Milo in her personal space so she doesn't have to worry about anyone else. She's got her chair angled towards him, and every so often she nudges her foot against the back of his knee.

"Not to be fucked up about it or anything," Penn picks up where Milo left off, "but I think I prefer those dudes. The ones who call while they're jackin' it." They accompany this with a jerking-off motion, just in case you missed it.

"It's definitely sexual harassment, but at least I can use the air horn on them. Plus they're easy to figure out in about two seconds. The *children*, however... Waste of time. Shouldn't they be bullying people online who ship something 'problematic'?" Penn mimes choking themself. "Like, stay off my landline."

"Did you meet another twenty-year-old baby gay at your last art show?" Dottie asks, because when Penn starts talking like this, you know that's exactly what happened.

Penn sighs, pushes their glasses up to rub their eyes, then lets the frames fall back into place as they get into it. "Yeah, you know that magazine mosaic I did? The 'Here and Queer' one. She told me, with her whole chest, that it was homophobic. I barely even blinked, I just very robotically told her that the whole 'queer is a slur' bullshit was mostly propagated by TERFs to force us to out ourselves more specifically, so then they could decide whether or not we were 'acceptable' queers."

Another mime-choke, and Artemis supplies the gag.

"As if nobody ever used 'gay' as a slur," he points out. "That was all the rage for us growing up, wasn't it?" A faux-wistful sigh. "Ah, the nineties."

"Cheers." Dottie lifts her glass and the rest of them follow.

"Anyway." Penn tosses back the rest of their drink. "I really said *propagated*, like, out loud for real, so you *know* at this point I'm just operating on autopilot with this shit. Propagated! And actually I don't even know if that's the right word, but it's too late. I've internalized it. It's part of me now."

"I swear some of these kids are worse than straight people." Artemis sighs. "Learn your own history, right? Google is free."

Dottie hums. "Some people are more worried about being 'woke' than being kind."

"Are they even woke, then?"

"No. It's performative."

"*Right*. Everything's a *gotcha!* moment, and they don't even *get it* to begin with. Cretins." Penn hops out of their seat. "What-ever, I'm getting drunk. Y'all need anything?"

No one does just yet, so Penn heads off, electric sliding or something like it to the beat of the Hayley Kiyoko playing on the speakers.

"I'm curious now..." Artemis looks at Stevie and Milo. "You think you two'll deal with all that noise? One look at you, people aren't gonna assume you're a queer couple."

"Yeah. I've dealt with that before," Stevie says before Milo can say I *have no idea*, because his lack of experience is such that he doesn't. "It's like, pretty much all the time? I'm with a guy, I'm straight. I'm with a girl, I'm a lesbian. Either way, I 'just haven't decided yet.' Just ask my mom."

She flicks her straw aside and drinks deeply straight from the glass. "Big fun."

Just ask my mom. Okay, so their earlier conversation has snapped *very* clearly into focus. Something for them to unpack later, Milo thinks, but thankfully Artemis doesn't dwell on the comment. He's always been good at picking up social cues.

Instead, he waves a finger between Milo and Stevie and says, "Oh, so that's why this works. The demis and bis have the same problem with the basic perception of their very existence."

Dottie looks at him, all amused incredulity. "You've been hanging around me too much."

"Nah, he's right," Milo goes along with it. "We're both mildly narcissistic, too, so, yeah, that's the main reason."

Artemis flicks his wrist in a dramatic *talk to the hand* motion. "Hush, you." He turns to Stevie. "You wanna hear something balls-to-the-wall *terrible*? It'll make you feel so much better."

Her smile is a little nervous. "I don't know how I'm supposed to resist."

"You're not." Artemis brushes off his shoulders, his pants, settles in. "So. When one of my aunties found out I was gay, she pulls me aside, and she asks me, 'How... do you have sex?'"

Milo and Dottie laugh. He's heard this story, and she was at the Thanksgiving dinner where it happened. Stevie covers her face, all secondhand embarrassment as Artemis continues with the utmost theatricality—hand gestures and wide eyes, gasps and perfectly timed pauses.

"Imagine my shock. My appall. I'm as speechless as I've ever been. I simply gape. And she says to me, *aghast*, as if I don't have the monopoly on that emotion at the moment"—pause for effect—"'*In the butt?* Oh. No. No, I wouldn't like that.' So."

He lounges back in his seat, picks up his drink. "That's how I found out Auntie Jo doesn't go for anal. And I have to think about that *ev-er-y* Sunday when she's playing 'Glory, Glory' or whatever on the church organ."

Stevie peeks at him from between her fingers. "I'm not sure that made me feel better at all."

"Sweetie pie, it doesn't make any of us feel better, I was just lying to you." Artemis pecks an air-kiss. "Real talk, though, it's fine. Dottie and I got lucky, our family's been cool as hell about everything. Confused sometimes, *Auntie* Jo, but cool."

"It's sad that it's lucky," Dottie admits. She gives Stevie's shoulder a soothing rub, like she knows all about whatever's up with the whole mom business (Milo's glad someone does, even if it's not him yet). "This is how it should go for everybody."

"Yeah." Stevie shifts in her seat. Milo puts his arm over the back of her chair. "Y'know, I think my favorite part of being queer is that it's *all we ever talk about.*"

"Well." Milo tilts his head back and forth, considering his own recent obsession with his sexuality and *what does it all mean?* existential dread. "Life is very hard."

"And we're trying to achieve self-actualization before the straights can take credit for it," Artemis adds. "You want some guy named Chad to have this kind of breakthrough?"

"I know a gay guy named Chad," Dottie says.

"No you *don't.*"

"What else is there to talk about?" Milo says before they can get into the Chad debate again (it's happened *a lot*, and always to no avail). "Sports? The stock market? Escrow? I don't even know what that means."

"No one knows," Artemis agrees. "It's mankind's greatest un-solved mystery."

"Right. And I don't want to be the kind of adult who only talks about their investment portfolio."

Stevie gives him an *oh, you big dummy* smile. "Millennials don't have *investment portfolios*, we have anxiety."

"Exactly why we do so many deep-dives into our *souls*," Milo tells her, "because we're just too painfully self-aware."

"Oh, fine," Stevie relents. Her smile widens, relaxes like it does whenever he says something to make her laugh. "I can't argue with you when you get all earnest."

"It's painful to watch," Artemis says. Milo makes a face at him.

"Do you *mind*, man, I think my girlfriend's seducing me."

"Can't believe you met someone who is so deeply into your cringe personality." Artemis winks at Stevie. "And on that note, no offense, honkies, but I'm capped on white people nonsense. My Black friends just got here. Dottie, you coming?"

"I'll catch up with you." She points to the ceiling to indicate the song that just started. "Hey, know what this reminds me of?"

"More white people nonsense?" Artemis offers, then dances his way across the floor, all flamboyance, before anyone can reply.

"'Good Vibrations,'" Stevie identifies the music, does some seemingly complex mental acrobatics—Milo sure doesn't know what's going on, anyway—and then says, "*Fear*, right?"

"Ugh, I love it when our brains are on the same wavelength." Dottie smiles indulgently. "One second Mark Wahlberg's white boy rapping and dropping his pants all over town, the next he's stalking Reese Witherspoon in *the* seminal erotic thriller of our youth."

"And fingering her on a rollercoaster," Stevie says.

"*Oh.*" Milo skates his fingers along one of Stevie's shoulder blades. "I remember that movie."

"Who could forget?" Dottie fans herself. "I'd probably let '96 Wahlberg finger me on a rollercoaster, too."

Stevie half-groans, half-laughs. "I can't play this game again. We did *two hours* last time. I think we've run out of celebrities."

"But Milo's never played. And I think it's good, you know, if he does." Dottie crosses her legs as if settling in for the ride. Milo imagines this is how she starts sessions with her clients. "You can figure out if this thing's really got the legs to last. Or if he has an irreconcilable fetish we don't know about."

"*Irreconcilable fetish,*" Milo parrots. "Are you allowed to say that, sex therapist?"

"You're not paying me, I'll say whatever I want."

Hm. Point to Dottie. Milo takes the bait. "Irreconcilable fetish like what?"

"Harry Styles," Dottie says, like she keeps that one in her back pocket. "Would you let him finger you on a rollercoaster?"

"I wouldn't *go* on a rollercoaster with Harry Styles. We'd get to the top and he'd try to make me freefall with him, bet. The dude's *whacky.*"

"Like Animal. From the Muppets," Stevie clarifies for Milo's inquisitively raised eyebrow. He *ah*'s and nods.

"See? That's smart," Dottie congratulates them both. "You guys can keep dating."

Milo puts his chin on Stevie's head, sighs. "I'm too demisexual for this."

She laughs, and Dottie says, "Boy, please. The 'Would You Let Them Finger You On a Rollercoaster?' game *transcends* sexuality. Example—wait for it—Idris Elba."

"Idris Elba could do anything he wanted to me on a rollercoaster," Milo says, and it's barely a thought before doing so. He sighs again, acquiescing to the girls' smug grins. How is he supposed to live like this? "Fine, I see your point."

"That's all I wanted to hear. Cheers," Dottie says again. She drains her drink and leaves them, sashaying away, to join Artemis.

Milo grins at Stevie. "*Aloooone* at last."

She gives him a funny look. "Are you going to murder me?"

"I mean, if you'll remember what you said about this song—" He hums a few bars of "I Think We're Alone Now," and snorts when she kicks him.

"It was an *observation*, not a suggestion!"

"I'm obviously not going to *murder you*."

"Said every white man ever."

"Oof. Okay, you know what, I'll give you that one." He takes a pull from his Shirley Temple (after sobering up from their earlier day-drinking, he volunteered to be designated driver tonight). "So, you doing okay?"

"Yeah. I'm just…" She gestures around at nothing. "Sorry if I'm being—"

"You're not being anything," he assures her when Stevie fails to articulate whatever she's thinking. He chucks her under the chin. "I just want to make sure you're okay."

"It's been a weird day," she sums up and leaves it at that.

It's not much, and it's the least Milo could have figured out on his own, but still he doesn't push. You can't make people talk about things; you just have to be there for them when they're ready to.

And he loves Stevie—don't hold your breath, he's not telling her that anytime soon (eventually, but not *soon*; he's figuring out how to be her boyfriend, they don't need any more pressure than that)—so of course he'll be there. In the meantime…

"Can I make it less weird?" he wants to know. "Or possibly more weird? I feel like our vibe is generally more weird."

"*Weeeeeell.*" Stevie's giving him those heart eyes that Milo doesn't think she *knows* she gives him (he's not going to tell her that, either, it'll only embarrass her). "Do you maybe have anything else you could tell me about lube?"

"Oh, she's got *jokes.*" Milo kisses her between the eyebrows. "No, actually, I think I ran through all the important parts with you the first time. Want me to ask you about your vaginal health?"

"How many details do you really want about my period?"

"Whatever you wanna tell me, baby face, I'm at your mercy."

"Such a *line,*" Stevie scoffs, the sound petering off into a giggle when Milo's next kiss lands on her mouth.

He keeps kissing her, too, because, *God*, does he like kissing her. Never done much of it before, he never really *got it*, you know? It just seemed sticky and wet for no reason, and like you were always expected to do something else, something more—kissing was always a prelude to *more*, and Milo had never been ready for it.

He's not ready for more now, either, but Stevie already knows that. She gets that. And it hasn't changed her mind about him.

So, yeah, kissing's still sticky and wet for no reason, but Milo likes doing it with her, anyway.

They go on like that for a while, kissing with no rush, public indecency and all—they're no Lars in the dog park, but *who is?*—but neither of them seem to mind the time or place. You have your first kiss in a grocery store, Milo figures you're not too fussed about making out wherever you feel like it. Besides, Stevie seems so on-edge tonight, he wants to make her feel better. If kissing's the way to go to distract her, he can do that. *Happily.*

That doesn't mean they get super handsy about it, though. That's just unpleasant to see in public, you can't do that to people. Milo just kisses her soft and slow and mostly keeps his tongue to himself, up until Stevie taps him on the hip to get his attention.

"Sorry," she says. "Bathroom."

Milo huffs a chuckle through his nose. One more kiss—one! He's not an *animal*, just a little (read: a lot) infatuated—before he pulls back.

"Do you want me to, uh. Come with?" Loretta's has two bathrooms, both unisex and single-stall. "Not in a pervy way."

"I'm okay. Could you get me another drink, though, maybe?"

"No. As you can see, I'm very busy." He plucks the glass from her hand. "Yeah, obviously I'll get you another one."

"You're so *funny.*"

"I'm choosing to not pick up on your tone," he decides, "so that I can pretend you mean that as a compliment."

She presses another giggle into his cheek, and off she goes.

The bar's a bit crowded, but Milo manages to hail Tatum—she knows precisely the ratio of vodka to lemonade that Stevie likes—and while he waits he chats with Penn, who's swapping streaming service info with Madison.

"Sharing is caring," they say. "I've tried the sugar daddy game, but for realsies I don't think I'm emotionally mature enough to really get into it. So how *else* am I supposed to fund my binge-watching, I ask you."

"Share passwords all you want," Milo supports them. "What am I, a cop?"

"I miss the early 2000s. I want to start pirating again."

"Mood."

Tatum slides a plastic cup across the bar and Milo trades her a ten, tells her to keep the change. He tells Penn and Madison he'll catch them later and they shoo him away, too busy recalling the specifics of their passwords to bother with pleasantries ("I can't remember if I capitalized the 'R' or not, Jesus Christ—").

Still no sign of Stevie. Milo goes back to where they'd been sitting, but there's nothing at the table but an ashtray and water rings. Hm. Probably there was a line for the bathrooms. Milo heads that way next.

Someone put the Tremeloes on the jukebox. A deviation from the synth-pop and dance mixes the usual crowd is into, with a few regularly scheduled exceptions (Dolly Parton, mostly).

But they get all sorts at Loretta's, and you can't deny that "Here Comes My Baby" makes you want to finger-snap and move your feet. Stevie's got this one across multiple playlists: *bangers*, *i don't want to talk about my ex*, and *if you need me i'll be dissociating to doo-wop* ("A lot of these aren't actually, *strictly* doo-wop, I just got excited").

Milo slips into the hallway by the bathrooms. There are a few people around, sharing ponytail holders and tampons and telling each other not to text that guy (it's usually a guy) who leaves them on read until he wants a blowjob. The usual.

The lighting's just as dim as the rest of the bar, but back here it's a normal color, so it's easier to see. And if Milo doesn't particularly *love* what he sees, well, that's a personal problem.

Stevie doesn't look like she's loving it, either, so there's a point for Milo's ego, with her crossed arms and the tight lines around her mouth while—cue the dramatic music, please—fucking *Erik* chats her up.

Erik. Fuck off, Milo had forgotten all about Erik.

Blissfully, naively, in the aftermath of his mostly-repressed feelings storm regarding the previous state of his love life, he hadn't thought to worry about Stevie's. And now here it is, barging in and sending him flying off the recliner all over again (metaphorically speaking this time, but *still*).

Life is just. So hilarious.

He's not sure what to do—Milo is not, by any stretch of the imagination, an *alpha male*—but he knows he can't leave Stevie here to deal with it by herself. That's not what he wants to do, anyway, he's not *useless*, so he strolls right on up to them like there's no anxious humming (screaming) going on his head.

Stevie relaxes when she sees him. And can Milo just pause here real quick to say that he loves that he can do that for her? When her tense muscles loosen up like her day's better just because he's in it. She makes him feel *important*.

"Libations," he says, and passes her the vodka lemonade. He puts his hand on her lower back, thumb stroking along the exposed skin that peeks between her shirt and sweats.

He's not doing it to be... *possessive*, Milo doesn't think. But then, maybe he's not thinking? All he knows is that Erik and his symmetrical face are movie-star charming, he somehow makes a popped collar look not ridiculous, and he knows how to talk his way into pants, into beds, into hearts (Milo's not sure how that last one happens, but the gossip mill says it's a total bummer to lots of girls who never manage to tame the playboy out of him, so, whatever floats your boat).

So, fine, maybe Milo's got another self-esteem issue or two to work out. The way Stevie smiles at him sure helps, though.

"Hey, man, how's it goin'?" Erik looks a little surprised, a little embarrassed, maybe, but Milo doesn't wonder at that. Most of the customers he runs into outside of Nobody's get pretty squirrely, like they think Milo's going to broadcast their deep dark sex secrets to the general population of Kroger, Speedway, or—on one memorable occasion—a child's birthday party.

(Imagine learning about your kid's godfather's balloon kink at FunFlatables, of all places. Yeah, no, Milo's not interested in that kind of responsibility.)

Unsure of what to say, he gives Erik a nod. Friendly enough, but not overmuch. See, Milo gets pretty squirrely, too, because how do you act around someone who routinely asks you for sex toy tips, but right now social norms dictate something entirely different?

There's a single beat of awkward silence before Stevie's had enough.

"So, um." She waves between them. "Milo, this is Erik, my—"

Ex-boyfriend? Ex-husband? *Current* husband? (*Oh, God.*) There's not enough time between Stevie's words for Milo to entertain all these possibilities, but he's making it work, until—

"—stepbrother."

GARTH BROOKS IMPRESSION I'VE GOT FRIENDS WITH LOW EXPECTATIONS

"**D**o you have *any idea* how worried I was?" Milo says, as if he's actually scandalized about the whole thing.

It's later that night, back from Loretta's after *serendipitously* (bah!) running into Erik. Stevie's had enough of her family for one day, so after making polite-ish excuses and ensuring their friends had rides home, she and Milo peaced out.

Erik hadn't done anything wrong. Neither had her mom. They just wanted to talk, catch up, whatever, and Stevie has a hard time explaining why that's hard to begin with. Milo hadn't pestered her about it, but she's going to have to explain it eventually, isn't she?

For now, they're at his place, digging into Chinese takeout across from each other at the kitchen island, under muted overhead lights and to the tune of Stevie's doo-wop playlist.

(Tatum had heavily implied she was bringing someone home tonight, and Stevie's still recovering from the whole Whitney thing, so, *no thanks*. Besides, Milo has *two* down comforters, which she's known from the first time she came over and maybe she's been trying to move in ever since.)

"How worried were you, Milo?" Stevie says now, like he set her up for a Johnny Carson exaggeration joke.

He stabs at a piece of orange chicken and points it at her. "*Distraught*. I thought you had sex with him!"

Stevie *blech*s. "That's just offensive."

"Because of the implications of pseudo-incest, or...?"

"Because it's *Erik*." Stevie spins too much chow mein around her plastic fork. Most of it falls off and she has to start over. "My hyperfixation in junior high was V.C. Andrews, I don't care about incest."

Milo props his chin in his hand, sighs dreamily. "You're so well-rounded."

"You're having way too much fun with this."

He laughs, straightens up and goes back to his food. "No, seriously, I *was* worried about it for a little bit. Just like, how's a guy supposed to compete? I think the dude's fucking ridiculous but apparently he's doing... *something*."

"I don't get it, either." Or, well, she does and she doesn't? It's the same sort of thing about Whitney—they suck, they just have this way about them where you don't notice it at first.

"I'd just kind of forgotten about him," Milo continues, "what with my own ex bullshit going on."

"I mean, I figured you guys must have crossed paths a couple times, but why would you think I had sex with him? It's not like I ever brought him up."

"That night I ran into you at Loretta's, you remember, it was after I wooed you with my extensive knowledge of lubes." He laughs again when Stevie blows a raspberry. "You and Dottie exchanged some *mysterious words* about him, so I made some assumptions."

"You could've just asked Dottie."

"I did ask Penn, but then, I dunno. I think maybe I didn't really want to know?" Milo chews thoughtfully, swallows. "And then it felt just, icky to be asking other people about your sex life. People get into that about mine all the time and I hate that, so I didn't want to turn around and do the same thing to you."

Stevie frowns at her noodles. There's nothing wrong with them, she's just getting in her head about everything. "Well, now I feel like an asshole for talking to Dottie about you."

"Nah." Milo waves her words away with his fork. "That's different. Dottie just, inherently understood the Whitney thing more than anyone else did, I think. You're the only person I ever told the whole truth to—yeah, you're very special, get that smug look off your face—but they knew it sucked. Dottie didn't want me to go through anything close to that again. And she knows you, so I don't think it was a thing where she thought you'd do that to me, but."

He scratches his cheek. "She wanted you to go into this with, like, a clear head, I guess."

"That's very insightful."

"Well, I'm a very sensitive person, Stevie."

"Hm." She scrunches her nose at him. "Then I'm glad we could put your anxious heart at ease with this whole Erik thing."

Milo exhales a deep whoosh. "Me too. If I'd been right, I'd be worried you still had things stuck inside you that have no business being there."

"Oh, right Speaking of." Stevie smirks. She can't help it, this is all suddenly completely hilarious. "You know how he's dating Madison? Yeah, she told me about the anal vibrator thing."

"Christ. Is she well?!"

"Physically, yes," Stevie assures him. She slurps at a noodle and it hits her on the nose. "He just asked her about it, I guess he didn't believe you."

"I am a God. Damn. *Professional*." Milo knocks his flimsy plastic fork against the counter with every word, until it snaps in half. He stares at it. "The *injustice*."

"You're such a drama queen."

"A goddamn *professional* drama queen," Milo corrects her. He gets up to grab another soda from the fridge, but swings the door shut in the next second, when The Impressions start to groove on Stevie's phone.

"*Don't—*" she starts to say, but it breaks off into laughter when Milo sings along over her protestations.

He's tone-deaf but enthusiastic, and he almost knows all the words. Stevie points her fork at him, a mostly useless threat. Milo snatches it and flings it across the counter; it lands in the sink—impressive—and he grabs her hand, pulls her to her feet so she'll dance with him.

"C'mon, baby, we're livin' out a Pinterest board dream here."

He waves at the far wall, where their shadows reflect in the dim golden light of the kitchen, and uses his other hand to spin Stevie in a circle. "See, right there, that's the picture."

It's been a weird day, all stress and cramps and repressed drama in her family dynamics (*hellooo*, growing up Irish Catholic).

It feels like a bunch of stuff she has to fix, but Stevie's not sure how to fix it, or the way she feels about it, but she probably can't do anything about any of it at one A.M. on a Saturday morning, so maybe she doesn't have to worry.

Because when Milo steps on her toes and sings off-key, laughing through the lyrics, Stevie thinks that maybe, actually, it's just like the song says—because right now?

Everything really does feel like it's all right.

***

...*aaaaaand* then it doesn't, in the approximate twelve hours it takes for her mom to call her again.

Stevie had made peace with the fact that Milo and Erik probably knew each other, but that was before Erik went full nosey snitch who told her mom *all about* "Stevie's new boyfriend who works at the sex store," who she just "*must* bring to the house so we can meet him, why didn't you tell us? Well, I'm not sure about this job of his, if I'm completely honest with you, Stevie, but even still of course we'd want to meet him!"

As if Stevie's (nonexistent) assumptions of their indifference and/or judgment was the reason she was keeping her mouth shut about Milo. Except for their respective Facebook statuses, but Stevie's parents don't have Facebook so it hadn't mattered.

But then, it doesn't surprise her that her mom doesn't get it. That's kind of always been the problem.

She'd known that, sooner or later, she would introduce Milo to her parents. She hadn't, however, expected that it wouldn't be on her terms, but rather at the whims of a frequent—and frequently, *laughably* worrisome—customer at Nobody's.

The fact that it just so happened to be the customer who is also Stevie's love-'em-and-leave-'em stepbrother only adds to the divine comedy of the whole thing.

Somebody had better be laughing, anyway, otherwise what is this all *for*?

If this thing with Milo keeps going the way Stevie wants it to—that is to say, for a long, long time (otherwise known as forever, but she feels like a cornball saying so)—then, yes, her family is an inevitability. But Stevie and Milo have only *just* gotten through Milo's hang-ups, and that had been hard enough on them both. Can't they just... *exist peacefully*? For like *five seconds*?

But no, of course they can't, because family dinner is the first Sunday of every month, and a new day (month) is *swiftly* dawning.

Stevie's gotten out of several of these get-togethers with the sometimes true, sometimes not, excuse of last-minute work deadlines. Her record is slim, just two months in a row before she feels like too much of an asshole to try ditching again. So, yes, she'd be going this Sunday, *anyway*, and theoretically it is *nice* to have Milo with her, but then again maybe not so much because now she's got to worry about him, too.

Stevie thanks her lucky stars that her wishes never came true and Erik's not dating Whitney, after all. Imagine the emotional turmoil.

Actually, she's trying to refrain. She has enough emotional turmoil to prepare for without creating senseless anxiety on top of that.

She repeats this to herself, over and over *endlessly*, on the drive to her parents'. Milo had plugged in the address and then put on Stevie's *frankie say relax* playlist (i.e., her calm-down songs) without her having to ask. She's barely said a word about how her family makes her feel, offered no deep explanation, but it must say something about the visible tension in her body that Milo just *knows*.

As usual, she's sitting criss-cross in the passenger seat, only now she's gripping her knees, spine almost painfully straight, to keep her airways open and make it easier to breathe. It makes her think of the first time Milo took her to the grocery store, when she accidentally panicked and he knew all the right things to do to help her.

Now, Stevie tilts her head to watch him through her aviators. Emily Kinney is crooning over the car speakers, and Milo's tapping his fingers to the beat in the open window. The way his arm's crooked, he's going to end up with a patch of sunburn on his elbow. He's wearing a sleeveless Springsteen concert tee (*swoon*) and his tie-dye headband, pushing back his curls that still whip around in the breeze without a care in the world—and the slight smile on his face that says he hasn't got one, either.

Maybe she won't have to worry about him too much today, then.

Like he can read her mind, his mouth twitches up a little more. "What's up, hot stuff?"

"My blood pressure."

"*Bah-dum-tss.*" Milo drums the steering wheel accordingly. "You take your meds today?"

"With food and everything."

"Good," he approves. "That's all you can do, baby face. If your parents suck, we'll just take all their potato salad and bounce."

She makes a gagging sound. "I don't like potato salad."

"It's not about the potato salad. It's about the *spite*."

"How are you this calm?"

"I have *never* been calm a day in my life and I *deeply resent* your implication." Another grin flashes across his face when Stevie groans at him. "Okay, honestly? I've never met anyone's parents before in, like, this capacity. I don't even know what to be worried about. Maybe if I wore a leather jacket or whatever, y'know, if I pulled the whole bad boy look, but I mean..."

He gestures down his front. There's a pink Slurpee stain on his shirt. "Look at me, I'm wholesome."

"Hm." Stevie supposes that's true, except—"Too bad they know about the dildos."

"Oh, ha, *ha*." Milo checks his mirrors at the intersection, then drives on. "So they know I'm gainfully employed. Dooooon't say it like I'm trafficking cock sleeves stuffed with hard drugs."

"Coke sleeves."

"Don't make *puns*, Stevie, it's unbecoming."

She sticks her tongue out at him, wiggles it suggestively to throw him off his game.

It works for about half a second before he laughs, delighted. "That's obscene. Oh, hey"—Milo points ahead to a rickety stand on the curb—"garlic pickles for sale. Interested?"

"I'm gonna have to hard pass on the roadside pickles," Stevie declines. "From a *shed*."

"Elitist."

She has to laugh. "*Elitist!*"

"You just want everything to be the world's biggest ball of yarn, otherwise it's not good enough for you."

"Five dollars for one pickle!"

"They're independent business owners!"

"Or serial killers," Stevie says, as if she's making a point, which, well, she really isn't. They've already driven past the place, besides.

Milo shakes his head. "Maybe we do watch too much SVU."

"Notice you didn't stop, though."

"Well, who has five dollars anymore?"

Stevie has to laugh again. It's true, it's funny, and she knows he's trying to distract her nerves with goofiness. She knows she loves him for it, too.

But all good things must come to an end, blah blah, and Stevie's nerves are back at it when the GPS announces *your destination is on the right.*

The house is a nice bi-level in a nice subdivision where everything looks pretty much the same. Most people do some-thing to stand out, so visitors can find them without going to the wrong house first: a mailbox shaped like something else (a dalmatian, a barn, a Cadillac), season-themed flags, an army of garden gnomes that get dressed up in toddler costumes on Halloween (if that sounds cute, Stevie can assure you, it's not), whatever does it for you.

Stevie's favorite is on the corner two doors down: a six-foot, inexplicably indestructible, stained-glass flamingo (his name is Gerald).

Rachel and Clark Callahan's is "the house that doesn't match" with its bright red door and robin's egg blue shutters, but it's thanks to that color scheme that their pizza never got delivered to the house around the block that has the same numerical address (11811), just a different street (South instead of North).

There's nothing wrong with any of it—except the gnomes, gotta admit she doesn't love the gnomes—but when Milo takes her hand on their walk up the driveway, Stevie doesn't think she could do this alone again. But maybe that's okay because now she doesn't have to.

Her mom looks like she always does—lovely, no-lipstick smile, ash blonde hair in a finely-done ponytail that's got a slight bounce, a slight curl at the end. There's a smudge of crinkles at the corners of her gray eyes. She's a little taller than Stevie, but most of that's in her discount-but-still-fashionable wedge sandals. All in all, a down-home kind of MILF, according to the boys Stevie went to high school with, and with whom Tatum agrees, so there's the gay/straight alliance for you.

Clark's got some Cary Grant thing going on, or so people say; Stevie's never seen the resemblance, but she's pretty sure that's just the default for any good-looking older guy. He's got a nice smile, too.

They're well-matched in looks and in temperament—both easy-going, in their own way, and neither prone to yelling.

Stevie reminds herself that she's lucky to have them.

It's very all-American family, but with no dark secrets lurking beneath that veneer. So, not quite as interesting, but they've got their own brand of problems, Stevie knows firsthand. The discovery of bodies in the finished basement or doctored birth certificates or proof of a second family the next town over would only belabor the point.

Point being, they just don't really *get* each other, but what family doesn't have that problem? Stevie tries not to complain.

(She doesn't try to deal with it, either, but come on—life isn't a heartwarming coming-of-age dramedy, there's no climactic argument that leads to a sudden understanding, reconciliation, promise to do better. No, you just learn to live with it, no matter how it makes you feel about yourself.)

They're so happy to see her, so right away Stevie feels like a supreme douchebag. It's not that she's *not* happy to see them, it's more that she's too anxious to have room for anything else.

It's the kind of anxious that gives her tunnel vision, where she can only focus on where this ends, when her nerves will be able to *relax* and this whole experience will feel like a fever dream. It's how it is when she has to go shopping: she operates on a tightly-coiled yet frenzied kind of autopilot until it's *done* and she can go home.

Introductions, small talk, Stevie's fingers itch for her Rubik's cube—pointless, because Clark always tries to very intensely explain the *physics* (???) of solving it to her—but Milo keeps holding her hand and that's just as good. Better, even. He's wearing one of those fidget rings on his thumb, so Stevie toys with that instead.

It's a nice day so Clark's going to grill, they're just waiting on Erik to get started (barbecues are all about the male bonding, Stevie's learned). Clark asks Milo if he grills often and Milo says "I'm gonna level with you here, sir, I don't trust myself that much around an open flame," ha ha ha, while Rachel tuts as she adjusts the strap of Stevie's Genesis tank top.

"I've got sunscreen, hon, otherwise you know you freckle something awful. Like a little Chuckie Finster, hm?"

Ha ha ha, *oh*, they have *fun*.

Stevie accepts a Bud Light—the Callahans' drink of choice, a measly 4.2% ABV but it'll have to do the trick—and so does Milo, despite his protestations that he's driving later, but Clark and

Rachel both say "But that's *later!*" and when neither of them are looking, Milo mouths a semi-horrified *peer pressure* at Stevie.

"Drink it slow," she mutters close to his ear, under the pretense of detangling a curl from his headband. "Or they *will* keep giving you another one."

"Good ol' Midwestern hospitality for ya," he mutters back, and kisses the worry wrinkle between her eyebrows.

They have a fenced-in yard and a spacious patio, where the shade cuts sharp, precise lines at the edges of the awning. It smells like grill smoke and citronella candles. The wicker furniture is cushioned with blue-patterned prints (always the same ones, whenever they need to be replaced). Milo sits with her on one of the loveseats, keeps his hand in her lap so she can play with his ring. Stevie almost spins it right off his finger when her mom asks how they met.

"At, uh, Loretta's," she says, hastily enough that you have to wonder if she's telling the truth. Which, of course, she's not. Stevie's not ashamed of the self-love, so to speak, but she's also not going to clue her parents in on her masturbation habits. There's healthy sexuality, and then there's healthy boundaries with family members.

More chit-chat that's less potentially invasive, so Stevie can calm down a little. Clark tunes into a classic rock station on the stereo, because the man can solve a Rubik's cube, allegedly, but music streaming's a no-go. Not that Stevie minds, duh, only she could live without the overzealous radio ads.

She gets a break—if you can call it that, considering—when her mom asks for help in the kitchen. Milo nabs her sunglasses to wear (he forgot his in the car), kisses Stevie's hand and pats her on the ass, he thinks he's funny and it shows in the corners of his smile.

"You're such a *boy*," she says with a playful roll of her eyes, because he's not at all.

"That's. Literally the worst thing anyone's ever said to me." But when she steps over his outstretched feet—just his sandals today, no socks—Milo slaps her butt again.

She was right earlier, to think that she wouldn't have to worry about him today. She's not even worried about leaving him on his own with Clark. Milo can talk to anyone, no problem.

Stevie, meanwhile, isn't sure she can talk to her own mother. They've just started slicing fruit when Rachel reminds her why.

"Now, don't get mad at me when I ask, but"—always a surefire way to make someone mad, but anyway—"is there something wrong with his..." Rachel taps a spot beneath her left eye.

Stevie takes a bracing breath, *quietly*, so her mom doesn't get defensive about her *attitude problem*. "Nothing's wrong with it. It's called strabismus. Milo's always had it, his has something to do with a muscle dysfunction."

"Well, I worry, I know he drove you both here."

Says the woman who force-fed him alcohol, but, sure. Stevie focuses on the thud of her knife on the cutting board, a smear of strawberry juice left over.

"The fact that he has a legally-obtained license probably should've made you feel pretty okay about it," Stevie replies dully. Her mom did ask her not to get mad, after all, and it's something Rachel asks of her a lot, so deadpan is her default.

Rachel laughs a little behind a close-lipped smile. It's both a relief and also incredibly condescending. "I was just *asking*."

"Okay." Slice and thud and strawberry juice. It's kind of nice, even though it makes her fingertips sticky.

"So." The shape of Rachel's mouth changes. "This job of his..."

Slice and thud, slice and thud, it's all very crisp and decisive and goal-oriented.

"It's not... you know... *prostitution*, is it?"

"Oh my God." Stevie drops the knife. "*Mom*."

"What?" Rachel cuts clean lines into a wedge of pineapple. "Erik said he works at a sex store, how am I supposed to know what that means?"

"He makes a living showing people how to put batteries in things the right way." That's not a guess, a joke, or an exaggeration; it's exactly what Milo says whenever he needs to explain, delicately, what he does.

It makes Rachel titter, like it's all very hush-hush scandalous. "Oh. Well, I didn't know!"

"Okay, but." Stevie sucks dried juice off her thumb. "That's a pretty, like, *ludicrous* leap."

Knowing Milo like she does, anyway, it's ludicrous. Stevie's not well-versed in why sex workers do their thing, only that those reasons have to vary just like any other job—but she doubts the option would even occur to Milo beyond a stale joke, and maybe not even then.

Rachel's arranging the cut fruit into neat shapes around her favorite ceramic platter (blue like the patio furniture, and *they didn't even come as a set, Stevie, so isn't that lucky?*). She says, "It's not like you tell me about who you're seeing. I thought that could be why."

Ah. So.

Well.

Stevie doesn't know what the fuck to do with that, actually. She picks at a strawberry stain on her thumbnail.

It bothers her, that her mom doesn't know *why*. Or that she's pretending not to know. Like she's fishing for something that Stevie doesn't want to give her, and she should know that. And if she doesn't know that, fine, but she should leave well enough alone. But, no, Rachel's never going to be satisfied until everyone's happy to her own personal standards of what that means.

God, Stevie lets her guard down for one second, and here she is, exactly where she didn't want to be. So never in her life has she been more relieved—or at all relieved! They're not that close!—to see Erik.

"'Sup, women?" He grunts slightly as he hefts another case of Bud Light onto the counter. He snaps the crease out of his polo shirt, then points over his shoulder. "Hey, Stevie, you know Madison. Rachel, Madison."

So that's still going on. Stevie waves and Madison waves back. Her dark hair is twisted into a long braid, frizzing along the edges, cornflower eyes etched expertly with coal, and little gingham dress tied with bows. She shifts a shy smile towards Rachel.

More small talk ensues—if Stevie has to hear *How was the drive?* one more time, swear to God, she's going to start walking everywhere, but at least it gives her a chance to chill.

She wasn't going to start an argument with her mom, there's never any point, but that pit in her gut opened up all the same and she hadn't been sure what to do with it. And she still doesn't know, but the interruption means she doesn't have to come up with anything.

Being here feels... off. Stifling. She doesn't feel like she can be herself; she doesn't even know how she'd start.

Because, the thing is, Stevie has her life. She has her routine, her friends, she's made herself comfortable. And maybe that doesn't sound like much, *comfort*, but it makes her happy, and nobody ever asks her *how*—the people she keeps around know exactly what she means. And even if they don't, they don't make a *thing* about it.

Stevie likes her freckles, her bad taste in vodka, she likes never giving a shit about FOMO because her couch is *really comfortable*, she likes Milo.

(She very probably definitely *loves* Milo, but one thing at a time.)

Nobody ever makes her feel like any of that's wrong. And then she's alone with her mom for the space of a single conversation and, no, it's not enough to make Stevie feel bad about any of that—just that she *should* feel bad.

It's not going to change anything. But it still pisses her off.

Rachel takes the fruit platter, tells Erik to grab the thawed burgers, and asks the girls if they'll collect a few more drinks and meet them outside.

Good. Another minute to get it together without locking herself in the bathroom. Stevie's a big believer in locking yourself in the bathroom, but if she does it now she's not coming out. She's learned to pick and choose her battles with her family, and the way she feels right now isn't worth causing a scene.

"Hey, so..." Just the two of them now, Madison nips at her bottom lip, shimmery with gloss. "Are you, like, mad at me or something? You seem kinda upset."

"No, I—" Stevie takes another one of those bracing breaths, only this time it feels like she can let go of some of the tension while she does it. "My family just stresses me out."

"Can I help? I mean, did I do something? Because I know you and Erik have the whole... thing," Madison decides, tactful. "I didn't mean to make it worse by being here."

Right. The *thing*. Well, that's a longer story than most people know, because all it ever did, really, was affect Stevie's own *thing*. It's nothing for Madison to worry about, and Stevie tells her so.

"No, it's okay. I'm glad you're here. Stuff with my family is like the only time I like it when a bunch of other people are around. I'm definitely not mad at you. About anything," Stevie reassures her as best she can because, hey, she knows how this goes. "I mean, *surprised*, yeah, that you're still with Erik after the whole vibrator thing—"

"Well—yeah, that was..."

"Appalling?" Stevie supplies.

Madison nods. "That's the word. And, okay, so I was kind of unsure about him at that point. I mean, a guy doesn't know the difference between your asshole and your vagina, you're going to have some questions, but..."

She shrugs, then backs it up. "I don't know. He's nice. He laughed about it, and then he apologized and everything. And it's not like he tried to just stick anything up there without my permission, you know? It's like I told you, he just didn't understand the big deal, so he asked me about it. I guess I figure, yeah, it was kinda dumb, but at least he asked."

Wow. The bar for straight boys is somehow lower than Stevie thought scientifically possible. She sees what Madison's saying, but at the same time, like... Jesus. What complete and total *bozos* has she dated that Erik's *orifice confusion* isn't an immediate red flag?

Oh, well. Madison's a big girl, she can make up her own mind about him. Just like with Tatum and Whitney, Stevie's in no hurry to give any advice.

Besides, from what she's heard, Erik's at least up front about his *intentions*. Sometimes his latest girlfriend thinks she can change his mind, sometimes she wants the same casual thing he does. Stevie can't be sure which category Madison falls under, but chances are she knows the score by now.

Carrying four beers each for the cooler outside, Stevie and Madison head back to the patio. Milo returns Stevie's aviators; they've already left a noticeable tan line to match the patch of sunburn on his elbow. She spritzes him with SPF 30, pats it dry and slightly sticky.

"Myyyy hero."

"Oh, are you gonna try groping my butt again?"

"Eh. I could probably get away with it." Milo bobs his head at Erik and Madison, who are macking on each other just this side of not-family-friendly. "The nerve. We gotta look at that *all day*."

"At least we have each other?"

"Baby face." Milo puts his hands over his heart. His smile is gooey. "You're absolutely wooing the shit outta me today, you know that?"

She spritzes his cheek with more Banana Boat and steals the rest of his beer, and the afternoon goes down a little easier from there.

Milo wraps Clark and Erik up into some conversation about cars she doesn't understand. Stevie ruffles his hair—he play-bites at her fingers—and leaves them to it.

Her mom dishes gossip about the ladies at church, to which Madison gets excited because she's heard conflicting accounts of the bake sale drama from a couple of her clients at the spa. They spend the afternoon piecing together The Events—*Patty said her grandson has a gluten allergy, but Mary Beth is married to Patty's grandson's doctor's brother-in-law, and apparently Patty is just on a health cleanse she doesn't understand, and Jean didn't even try to pass the store-bought doughnuts off as her own and she said gluten isn't real when Patty complained, and then...,* on and on—like amateur detectives with a hunch and a dream. Stevie dutifully takes notes on her phone.

They don't get anywhere substantial, but all the same it's a nicer time than Stevie expected to have.

She even starts to think, hey, this isn't so bad. Maybe she won't have to skip these get-togethers at all anymore, so long as Milo's with her (she thinks he always will be) and another two-or-more people show up. It might not be ideal, but it's *okay.* She can do this.

It's going on six-thirty when they pack it in. Nearly four hours with her family without a meltdown, without locking herself in the bathroom to decompress even once. Stevie's actually going to get out of here without crying, without *wanting to.*

And then her mom pulls her into a hug and ruins everything.

A kiss on the cheek and a heartbreakingly *relieved* hum in her ear—"I'm just so happy you met somebody, honey."

That's it, and all her good feelings are kaput.

That's it, and it shouldn't ruin *anything*—it shouldn't but it does, and that just makes it worse.

In the car, Stevie tucks her head between her knees and starts to cry. She hears Milo say "Oh, shit" through a panicked laugh that's not really a laugh at all, and then he's rubbing her back in sweeping, soothing circles.

"I'm sorry." She sniffs. "I'm sorry, I'm just bursting into tears out of nowhere—"

"Not really out of nowhere," Milo assures her. "Though, I *will admit!* I don't know why you're crying, but. Yeah. I could tell you wanted to."

So she wasn't as well-adjusted as she thought. Stevie keeps her face tucked away when she asks, "You could? I did?"

"Pretty much all day, actually, so the fact that you lasted this long, well, clearly you've gone and emotionally stunted yourself."

She hiccups through a laugh. "Shut up."

"*You* shut up." His hand makes one more pass through her topknotted hair before he pulls away, and Audrey II rumbles to life. "I'm gonna get you a Slurpee."

"What? Why?"

"You once implied a seventy-two-ounce Slurpee gets your rocks off, and I hear orgasms are good for a mood boost." The car rolls smoothly over the paved streets and Milo rambles on. "Now, I am in no position to fuck the sad out of you—in fact I'd probably make things worse, just because I know which vibrator to recommend for G-spot stimulation—the Womanizer Duo, by the way, nobody's ever said no to that one, and also I think the We-Vibe Chorus saved this one couple's marriage, I can't be sure but they literally sent an Edible Arrangements to the store like two weeks later, so, far be it from me to cast judgment upon whatever the fuck was going on there, but *anyway*..."

He coughs. "That does *not* mean I have any rhythm in my hips whatsoever, like, I'd have to hum 'Another One Bites the Dust' to even try to keep the beat, and y'know I think that might ruin the moment?"

Stevie's not shaking with tears anymore, but with irrepressible giggles that make her stomach ache in the good way.

She sits up straight, lets the blood rush to all the right places in her body, still laughing but it doesn't hurt so much now that she's not folded in on herself. Most things feel better when she's not like that, and it *all* feels better when she's with Milo.

They're at a stop sign, so he looks at her—he usually stays focused on the road, but he looks at her whenever he can—and he's got that flicker in his eyes, in the soft curve of his smile, the flicker that says *Just shut up and let me love the sad out of you, huh?*

Stevie doesn't know how she knows that, she couldn't explain it. But she does. There's only one thing she doesn't know what it comes to Milo, really, and that's just...

How have they only just gotten started with each other? How hasn't she known him forever?

God, she needs to start saying this stuff to him more.

The 7-Eleven parking lot is crowded but not too much. Milo finds a spot by the curb. He pops the glovebox and hands Stevie a pile of fast-food napkins, kisses her cheek and says he'll be right back. And there he is, in record time, with the promised seventy-two ounces—cherry limeade for him, orange creamsicle for her—and he's licking the side of his cup where it overflowed. "Clearly I can't be trusted."

They open the tailgate and sit there, feet swinging—Stevie's swing, anyway, and Milo's skim over the gravel—as they suck on purple plastic straws and get ready to talk about their feelings again.

As far as relationships go, Stevie's pretty sure she has the best kind with Milo. The right kind. Meant-to-be and everything.

The parking lot smells like gasoline and fried food. Huey Lewis and the News jams over the staticky speakers. The air is humid and still, but snatches of laughter, conversation, revved engines, get caught in it just as easy as they would on a cool breeze. Milo's thigh is pressed against hers, and their ankles knock together every time they swing their feet.

It's kind of perfect, you know?

Stevie doesn't want to spoil it. But. She looks at Milo, the sunburn on his cheeks and shoulders, at his goofy grin when he sticks his tongue out at her, stained artificial red, and she doesn't think there's anything at all that could spoil them.

She thinks about what her mom said—*I'm just so happy you met somebody.* As if Stevie's never met anyone before. As if she's never wanted her parents to meet her *someone.*

She hasn't for a long time, but she *had*, once.

And, sure, that person hadn't been Stevie's someone, after all; no, her *someone* is sitting next to her right now and he's not going anywhere—Milo told her that, he *proved* that. Stevie thinks it's high time she gives him something in return.

So, she tells him about her first serious girlfriend, the first one that felt *real*, about Ashlee Thompson, with her crooked front teeth and the Facebook she only used for those memes that have Minions on them for no reason, the kind grandmas post like it's some kind of secret grandma code.

What else can she say, Stevie thought it was cute. Sometimes that's all it takes.

They were together for six months before Stevie worked up the nerve to tell her parents—"And it's not like they said anything, they didn't tell me no, but my mom... She'd met a couple of my boyfriends in high school and she couldn't have loved them more. I could tell it was different this time."

Chalk that up to another thing Stevie knows but doesn't know how to explain. You just feel it, when your mom's disappointed but she doesn't want to say so.

Stevie can still feel it like it's still happening, but she doesn't want to linger on it. Doesn't want to linger on any of this, doesn't want to overthink it, so she keeps going.

She never did introduce Ashlee to her parents. Maybe she would have, maybe she wouldn't have, Stevie was balancing the pros and cons when Ashlee broke up with her—"We got our wires crossed, I guess? I thought we were serious, exclusive, whatever. She didn't. It wasn't something she wanted, she was on and off with a couple of other people, too. Which—well, it sucked at the time, but then I found out one of those people was Erik, and... yeah. I mean. *That.* Who sees that coming?"

None of them had realized it, it wasn't something Ashlee or Erik had done on purpose. But they didn't break up, either; then again, they didn't need to once Ashlee ended things with Stevie.

Gosh, it had just... It was a mess. Stevie can't help but laugh a little bit about it now, even though it's not funny.

She's talking and Milo never interrupts, not even a sniff, a cough, an *um*. It's different than when they'd talked about his past; that had been a *conversation.*

This, though, this is something that's only fair for him to know, but Stevie just wants to get through it. If she doesn't shut down when she's talking about her mom, there's no way she could get through talking about her.

Because that's what it all comes back to, when Erik was the one who brought Ashlee home.

That had been a slice of hot goss for their college friends. Still is. Even now, a handful of years later, everyone—whether they were around at the time or not, but by now it's fairly common knowledge in their circles, it's part of their archived history—thinks her family stuff is because Erik dated her ex. Stevie lets them, because she doesn't want to talk about the *actual* problem.

"It wasn't even about Ashlee," she tells Milo now. He's the only one she wants to tell the whole truth to, the only person she thinks will get it the way she needs him to. "Like, yeah, it was stupid and dramatic at the time, we were like, nineteen? So for a while I thought I was just mad about that."

She looks at her lap. Her Slurpee cup sweated water stains into the frayed knees of her jeans. "And I was mad at them both, don't get me wrong. But it was more that our parents were so *excited* for Erik, but when I'd wanted them to meet her... It just wasn't the same. And I don't think it ever would be. And that still matters, you know? Maybe it seems like it shouldn't, because I'm with you and you're a guy, but I'm still bi. And that's"—she swallows—"it's not real to them."

"*Baby*." Milo's voice is coated in affection, in care. "Of course that still matters."

When Stevie looks up at him, Milo wastes no time in cradling her cheek. His hand is cold from his own cup.

"They should be happy when you're happy, whatever that looks like. If that's conditional for them... I mean, c'mon." He does that lip-flapping thing horses do. "That's not how it should be. It's fucked up."

"I think so, too." She can feel how sad her smile is. Milo strokes the edge of it with his thumb. "I know they love me, which is, you know, it's more than a lot of people can say about their family when they come out. Maybe that's why I don't really talk about it, because it could be worse and I should be grateful that it's not. And I am, it just..."

Her gaze flickers down, to that chapped corner of Milo's mouth he can never seem to smooth out.

"I don't know," she decides, without actually deciding anything. "It still hurts."

"I know it does." Milo dips his head to catch her eye. "It's like, just because things could be worse doesn't mean they're *right*, either."

See, she knew he'd get it.

When she nuzzles comfortably into his neck, Milo's arm winds around her, nudging her further into him. He smells like sweat and sunscreen. He kisses her hair at the temple, where Stevie's sure she smells like sweat and sunscreen, too.

"I'm sorry I didn't talk to you about this before," she says. "Or—I know we touched on it, I guess, but I didn't talk to you about it enough. I should've like, *explicitly* warned you."

"Ah, well." Another kiss, and Milo leans back to take a draw from his Slurpee, arm still around her shoulders. "We were a little preoccupied with my emotional spiral, weren't we?"

He snaps his fingers, does a little shimmy. "One identity crisis at a time, baby."

"*Maybe.*" Stevie's smile doesn't feel so sad anymore; it's still a little more so than a smile should be, but she's getting there.

She stirs her straw around the mushy, melting ice in her cup. "But still, I should be more... *open* with you. You are with me."

"I don't know about that." He strokes her arm, fingertips skimming up and down. "I think, like, we don't always know how we feel until something makes us feel some kind of way, you know? Or—I don't know if I'm putting this right."

Milo scrunches his face, squinting at the sun as he thinks. "I guess it's just, like, it's hard to lay it all out on the table. It's overwhelming. I don't expect you to tell me everything about you in one sitting. I sure as shit don't know everything about *myself*, even. I think the best we can do is take it as it comes." He taps her arm, twirls his wrist, palm flat as he cuts through the humid air. "Just roll with it."

Stevie knocks her forehead against his shoulder. "*How* do you always know the right thing to say?"

"Oh, it's an *evolved* survival skill." Milo's chest shudders with held-back chuckles. "You get enough dudes asking about size versus girth, you learn to say the right thing."

"*Jeez.*" Stevie plants an amused scoff in the crook of his neck. "What do you tell them?"

"Technique." Milo bops her nose. "Above all else."

"*Dreamy,*" she teases, but she means it, too.

"I've got fuck-all personal experience with sex, *as you know*, but you know something else, baby face?" He tilts her chin up, gives it a tap. "It's all about the effort. I figured that out when you showed up, and I'm learning how *fucking rad* it is to just... try."

Stevie smiles at him, all Slurpee sugar, nothing sad about it anymore. They've still got a ways to go, but Milo's right—you can't know everything all at once, you can't do it all at the same time. Sometimes there's no solution and you just have to roll with it as it comes. Sometimes things change and nothing's a straight line, point A to point B.

All you can do is try to get there, wherever *there* is, with whoever else is trying to get there, too. So if the only thing Stevie knows is that Milo's going her way, then she knows enough.

"Yeah." She loops an arm around his waist, hugs him close, and he hugs her back just the same. "I think I'm learning that, too."

CUE THE '80S POP FADE-OUT

A nother day, another thousand weird things happening at your local strip mall sex store.

This isn't quite the path Milo chose through the lens of his childhood dreams (he'd been thinking more along the lines of cowboy, but that probably wouldn't have worked out, seeing as he's got the upper body strength of a worm on a string—and thank you, Dottie, for *that* unforgettable comparison), but it is the one that keeps him in brand-name Pepsi, so them's the breaks, kid.

And today, the *breaks* include:

- An older woman in very pink lipstick, a sunhat, and *Life's A Beach!* tee, visibly concerned (really owning that T-shirt's double entendre there) as she inspects the original Magic Wand and asks Milo, "You're supposed to put this *inside yourself*?" Gotta admit, he didn't expect that, so he replies, equally concerned, "What? No. Jesus. Wands are external use only. *Only*-only. Pretty great for a back massage, too, it doesn't even have to be a sex thing." She buys it, so it's not for nothing.

- A gaggle of dancers who flick through the lingerie and costume racks and buy out a solid third of stock.

Dancers get a twenty-percent discount, but they tend to spend upwards of a hundred bucks, anyway. Milo wishes they wouldn't pay in *singles*—yeah, obviously he knows that's how they get their tips, but like... Go?? To the bank?? He has to *count* that.

- Some guy in a suit selling homemade banana bread. Milo doesn't know what to do with this, so he pretends to have a banana allergy.

- Definitely a tri-town football mom. Her name is Betty and she has an appointment at the salon down the street to get her roots done, but she's got some time to kill so she thought, *Oh, why not?* and here she is. She has *a lot* of questions about the BDSM wall, the answers to which she finds *delightful*. She stacks every product she asks about in her arms, saying every time, "Oh, this is *hysterical*, I just have to—" until she ponies up three hundred bucks. Talk about committing to the bit. Milo wishes her nothing but good fortune on her journey.

Lars comes through and thanks Milo for the "leave your curtains open" idea (Milo politely requests that Lars never say anything like that to him ever again, thank you).

Bryce stops by, too, to drop some primo cash on a Fleshlight because "I gotta take a break from chicks for a while, man, it's not worth the hassle," so it would seem that his girlfriend did indeed break up with him for sucking, and not the way she wants. Probably good for her overall health, because when Milo asks Bryce if he wants to add any toy cleaner to his purchase, Bryce gives him this *look* and says, "What do I need to clean it for?"

So. Just your average day at the office.

Not long before it's over, Erik shows up, thereby completing Milo's Bermuda Triangle of men who say the worst things you've ever heard in your life.

Upholding that reputation, Erik indicates the front rack of men's toys and asks, "What's a prostate stimulator?"

"The answer is in the question," Milo quotes. (He's not sure *what* he's quoting, but that's definitely a quote, right?)

"Isn't that kinda..." Erik drops his voice to a whisper. "For gay dudes?"

"It's for anyone with a prostate, Erik."

He makes a face like that can't be right. This *is* the same guy who thought he should use an anal vibrator on someone's vagina—prayer circle for Madison, everyone!—so Milo isn't all that surprised.

But Erik is full of surprises, anyway, when he clears his throat and gets to what is apparently the point of his visit. "So, uh. How's Stevie?"

Okay. This is a potential minefield. Milo can't decide how to cross it, so he goes for as honest as he can. "...Fine?"

Erik sighs, annoyed. Milo is genuinely a little bit offended.

But maybe the annoyance is for himself, the situation, maybe it's not personal. Erik won't look at him as he talks, instead tidying up a row of single-use masturbators (and *yes*, that really does mean you can use it *just one time*, you *filthy animal*).

(...also, yes, Milo would be the first to admit that talking to his girlfriend's stepbrother while the guy distracts himself from his own vulnerability with The Fun Factory Manta Penis Vibrator—*not* single-use, but you still have to *clean it*, Bryce—is pretty strange fare for your day job.)

"Look, Milo, I know I'm a dumb guy," Erik says, like it doesn't mean dick to him. "But me and Stevie... Our parents got married when we were teenagers, so I know her kind of well but also, like, not at all. But I know when her mom gets to her. And I know it bums her mom out when Stevie doesn't come around to visit. So, vicious cycle, right?"

Ah. This has taken a turn into the unexpectedly insightful, brought to you by Erik Callahan. Milo thinks he preferred the minefield.

"Yeah," he agrees, "I guess it would be."

"Okay. So." Erik scuffs his shoe against the laminate wood, leaves a mark. "Is she cool?"

Milo kicks his foot aside to rub out the streak with his own shoe, lest Cooper have an aneurysm about it later. "She's alright. I'm working on it."

Erik nods, satisfied, and that's it. Not exactly an after-school special heart-to-heart, but it's *something*.

And maybe Stevie wants that kind of something from her mom, but after what she explained to Milo a few weeks ago? She could use this vague impression of a heart-to-heart from Erik, too. This is a start, there's an effort happening. Milo wonders what Erik's take is on the whole Ashlee situation, if he realized anything was wrong, if he even remembers it now.

It's not Milo's place to step in that. Right now he's just trying to let Stevie feel her feelings, and things are going good. As for everything else...

They'll figure it out. But they don't have to do it right now.

In fact, Milo has very determinedly decided that they're not doing any more emotional labor for like, two weeks. Maybe three.

He hasn't nailed down the timeline yet, he still has to talk to Stevie, but! The two of them? Yeah, they're taking a goddamn *break*.

After his shift at the auto shop on Sunday, Milo left Audrey II there for a tune-up. With what he's got planned, his boss said he'd take a look to make sure Milo was good to go.

Today, after closing the morning drawer and saluting Penn goodbye, he meets Stevie in the parking lot.

She's sitting on the hood of Tatum's borrowed car, enjoying the breeze coming off the late afternoon sky. The sun picks out the light blonde in her hair, making all the frizzy bits shimmer. Her aviators are pushed up over her headband, and she's wearing Milo's old high school gym shirt (the thing's immortal) and those leggings with the bleach stains. The bumblebee Crocs are disposed of on the pavement in front of her.

Chin in her hand, Stevie grins when she sees him. It sends off that thrum in his heart that's both all too familiar and something he'll never get used to.

He hops off the curb and jogs towards her.

"So!" Milo claps his hands as he skids to a stop in front of her. Runs into her a little bit, too, as Stevie slides off the car and slips her shoes on. "Ouch, sorry—so—I've been thinking—"

"Don't hurt yourself."

"Uh, thanks, *Artemis*."

She is *entirely* too pleased with herself for that one. "Okay, Milo, what have you been thinking about?"

"Your work schedule."

Her face falls. "Yeah, I—I know I've been overdoing it. It's just, it's all this excess energy after seeing my mom? I don't know, I always kind of bury myself in projects after I see her."

"Hey, that's okay," Milo assures her. "I'm not *lecturing you* about your coping mechanisms, Dottie would never let me see the light of day again, no, I just—you're like, what, a whole month ahead of your to-do list?"

"Unless anything last-minute comes up, yeah."

"But you can work from anywhere."

"Yeah..."

"And I've blocked out my vacation time starting in"—Milo lifts a hand, counts down on his fingers—"one-two-three days. So I was *thinking*, if you're *amenable*..."

Milo pauses to take a breath, partly for dramatic effect but also mostly because he's nervous.

"Why don't we trap ourselves in a car together for two weeks? Ish. Two and a half? We'll see. But, yeah, really put this relationship to the test," he jokes, still nervous, *more* nervous. "And, yeah, obviously there will be low-budget hotels involved, we're both *far and away* too delicate to live without indoor plumbing, but, uh."

He tilts back and forth on his feet. "We could really knock out a few roadside attractions in two weeks, y'know. I looked at a map and everything."

Stevie blinks at him. Not quite the reaction he was expecting, but! That's okay! Maybe she just needs a minute. It's not like Milo's ever been at a loss for words, he can keep talking until she catches up.

"And, look, I'm not a millionaire—maybe if Nobody's was high-end and we could've been trusted with, like, The Royal Pearl? Or any of those 24k gold dildos, that commission would be pretty, y'know..." Milo whistles. "But! Not the case, so we're stuck in the Midwest for our totally righteous tour of roadside attractions.

"So, like, the Fremont Troll is out—for now!—but we've got ketchup bottles, we've got balls of paint, we've got the Santa Claus Village that for some reason I can't explain but I have this niggling suspicion that it's turned into, like, this den of debauchery, I guess we'll find out when we get there—oh!"

He snaps his fingers. It's a good thing he wrote all these down, or his excitement would've shaken all the pertinent information loose by now. "And we've got Iowa's largest frying pan—not *the world*'s, just Iowa's, but we could all learn a little lesson in humility, I think, so—"

Stevie takes a single step into his personal space, and she cuts him off with a kiss.

Ah. See, *that's* the reaction he was going for. Milo melts into it, and everything else he was going to say drips off his tongue.

Except—because this part's important, so he mumbles it against her lips—"We've even got the world's biggest ball of twine that started this whole thing."

"The world's *alleged* biggest." Stevie pecks him one more time before dropping back to the flats of her feet. Milo puts his hands on her hips, squeezes.

"Have a little *faith*, sweetheart."

And be still his *heart*, that smile of hers is just *yowza*. She tugs on his collar. "What else do we have?"

"Ball of stamps, *several* disconcerting statues…" Milo ticks off on his fingers, then wiggles them. "And I'm still trying to figure out a way to trick you into the hair museum."

"*Trick* me?"

"I was trying to make it as skeevy as possible." He slots his hands into the dips of Stevie's waist, then adds, conspiratorially, "It's what the hair museum deserves."

She holds onto his waist, too, gives it her own squeeze. "You've kinda just shown your hand here."

"Well, that's because I find you irresistible."

Her smile brightens, hearts in her eyes, the whole thing, and, yeah—*irresistible* sure covers it.

Milo figured this trip would be good for them. Not that they're having problems, it's not that; it's that they both deserve to have a good time. And they've always had fun together, but now they can actually, properly *enjoy* the fun, without having some kind of personal crisis panic about it.

Because now they've *talked*, they've had their first meltdowns with each other and they've figured out how to keep going from there. It's a lot of Slurpees and sodas and cuddling, and really what's better than an obscenely large beverage and holding hands with your number one?

Hey, Milo doesn't need a lot.

And when Stevie hugs him tight, giggling into his shirtfront and bouncing on her toes, telling him, *Fine! I'll go to the hair museum!*, Milo's got absolutely *everything* he needs.

***

A week later and with the not-a-threat-but-a-promise from their friends that "I swear to God, if you guys get married in some roadside chapel without us, I will start screaming and never stop," they pack their bags into Audrey II at a perfectly reasonable ten A.M.

The weather's all clear skies and the traffic should be light, they'll swing by 7-Eleven to spend too much of their budget on gas station snacks, and, of course, they've got no shortage of road trip music to get them through the next few weeks.

They're just about to pull out of Stevie's driveway when she gets them started with *bangers*. The first shuffle goes tooooooo—

Starship. "Nothing's Gonna Stop Us Now."

"Christ." Milo twists the key in the ignition, purple rabbit's foot (the fake kind, the real ones freak him out) swaying to the beat. "Maybe my life really is a rejected John Hughes script."

"*Rejected*?" Stevie echoes, like the mere suggestion alone is unfathomably offensive to her. What a doll.

"Well, there's no accounting for taste. But, c'mon"—Milo flicks his sunglasses down to look at her—"you *know* Hollywood would only greenlight it if you popped my cherry first."

"Ask me to prom and I'll give you the ride of your life," Stevie says, with no enthusiasm whatsoever, except for the very slight twitch in her lips when Milo laughs.

He flips his sunglasses back into place. "*Romance* me, why don't you."

She spreads her hands. "I'm fresh out of moves, Milo."

"Oh, I don't believe *that* shit for a second." Milo tosses her a wink that she can't see through his lenses, so he adds that tell-tale click of his tongue so she'll catch his drift. Stevie scrunches her nose at him—*nailed it*—and he gives it a tweak.

"Just remember, baby face," he tells her as they hit the road, "when it comes to you, I'm a sure thing."

Acknowledgements

With all the love in my body (which is a lot, I'm pretty tall), to:

- Melissa, Meg, and Gus, because you've routinely seen me at my Absolute Worst—aka when I go full obsessive over my work—and you're still around. What is wrong with you. Unconditional love? Get out of here.

- Alie, for the music; Haley, for all the heart-eyes emoji enthusiasm; May, for every unhinged DM when I am the least emotionally prepared for it; and Laura, for always Getting It.

- Casey, who makes me feel more impressive than I am; and Craig, for supplying the vodka it took for me to finish the first draft.

- Nikki, Emily, and the night of "Would You Let Them Finger You On a Rollercoaster?" And for Hanna, because I know you're gonna accidentally buy, just, so *many* copies.

- Siren, for the years of Pretentious Literary Chats that have imprinted on my very soul. And Katie, because all our teenage influences did the same thing.

- Mandy, Al, and Bekah, for all of that bammin' slammin' bootylicious wlw energy.

- Kirstin and Amanda, who are at once my biggest fans and soft marshmallow people who won't yell at me to hurry up and finish writing, even when I ask them to; and Woodsy, who actually did capslocks at me, and completely unprompted, too.

- And to everyone who reads and loves my stuff, everyone who's rooting for me: Keep it comin'!! I need those vibes to live!!!

About the Author

Kat Majik is actually three knockoff Muppets in a trench coat. One of them waterfalls caffeinated beverages and contributes nothing, while the other two debate the merits of em dashes versus parentheses. They compromise by overusing both and calling it *aesthetic*. And, eventually, they get around to finishing a book.

Stay up to date with all her book progress and other musings at linktr.ee/katmajik.

The cover designer, Meg, is open for commissions. Get in touch on Twitter, Bluesky, and Ko-fi @redbelles, and/or via the author's contact info.

Made in the USA
Las Vegas, NV
13 December 2024

14058546R00152